TIME AND GINGER

BY RONALD ALEXANDER
ACTING EDITION

DRAMATISTS
PLAY SERVICE
INC.

SOUND EFFECTS RECORD

The following sound effects record, which may be used in connection with production of this play, can be obtained from Thomas J. Valentino, Inc., 151 West 46th Street, New York, N. Y. 10036.

No. 5025—Telephone ring, door bell

CHARACTERS
(In order of appearance)

EDWINA (WINNIE) DAVIS
VIRGINIA CAROL (GINGER) DAVIS
EDWIN (EDDIE) DAVIS
TINKER DAVIS
BILLIE GREY
SAM GRAHAM
HOWARD CAROL

SYNOPSIS OF SCENES

ACT ONE

SCENE 1—The Davis living room. Afternoon.
SCENE 2—The same. Three hours later.

ACT TWO

SCENE 1—The same. Later the same day.
SCENE 2—The same. Two days later.

TIME AND GINGER

ACT ONE

SCENE 1

SETTING: *The living room of Mr. and Mrs. Edwin Davis. Everything about the room has the striking appearance of deja-vu. It is as though most of us have been there before, and indeed, many of us have since it is the former home of Mr. and Mrs. Howard Carol of "Time Out For Ginger" fame. The home is now inhabited by their daughter, Virginia (Ginger), her husband Eddie and their two grown children, Edwina and Tinker. The physical structure of the room is exactly as it was when seen some thirty years ago. The main features being the entrance hallway Center Stage that leads to the unseen outside door. In the entrance Stage Left is a flight of steps leading to the second floor. In the wall Right is a large window which is the main source of light for the room. In the wall Left is a swinging door that leads to the kitchen. The room is traditionally and properly furnished with the obligation that the sofa and coffee table by Down Center Right near the window and a large arm chair and ottoman be placed Left Center so as to have as much playing space as possible and not impede the action of the play.*

AT RISE: *Edwina Davis, (known as "Winnie"), a beautiful, lean twenty-one year old, is in the last stages of hanging curtains on the window Downstage Right. The front door slams offstage and Virginia Carol Davis (known as "Ginger", or Virginia, or Mrs. Davis) appears in the hallway. Ginger carries an attache case which she places on the coffee table Downstage Right.*

GINGER. Hia, Winnie.
WINNIE. Hi.
GINGER. Curtains look nice.
WINNIE. I think so. How do you like the windows?
GINGER. They look great. You can see right through them.

WINNIE. (*Nods.*) That's because they have no glass in them.

GINGER. How come?

WINNIE. Your son decided to wash them. He put up a ladder outside, and the next thing I knew, he and the window were lying all over the living room.

GINGER. He's always been a little flighty.

WINNIE. A little flighty? He's one flap away from being a butterfly.

GINGER. I know. But I keep hoping he'll outgrow it.

WINNIE. There are some things young men don't outgrow after they've turned sweet sixteen.

GINGER. But, maybe if nobody else notices, he won't either.

WINNIE. I don't see how that's possible, since he's practically engaged to the boy next door.

GINGER. (*Flat.*) The boy next door, happens to be a *girl*.

WINNIE. In drag.

GINGER. How can you say that? Billie Grey is a very pretty sixteen-year-old child.

WINNIE. Or a thirty-year-old transsexual, I'm not sure which.

GINGER. She just comes on a little strong.

WINNIE. A *little strong*? She's off the wall. Last night, she drove him home and walked him to the door. They stood outside for half an hour. Then I heard him squeal, and she said, Why are you so uptight, Babes!

GINGER. (*Takes a long beat.*) My God—she calls him "babes"?

WINNIE. (*Nods.*) Yes. "Babes and Billie," the Barbie dolls. I wonder why she changed her name from William.

GINGER. (*Shrugs.*) Your name is Edwina.

WINNIE. I know. Your generation certainly had the cutes when it came to naming children. *Edwina* and *Tinker*.

GINGER. Not really . . . Tinker was my mother's maiden name.

WINNIE. Who's to blame for Edwina?

GINGER. Your father. He was so sure you were going to be a boy, the only name he could think of was Edwin.

WINNIE. *Junior.*

GINGER. That's right. Even after they showed him you were a girl, he called you Eddie for three days.

WINNIE. That's a pretty kinky comment on your relationship.

GINGER. Maybe. But that's the way he was programmed. He wanted a boy child to carry on the tradition.

WINNIE. Dad went to a military institute for four years, studied engineering, and was engaged to my dizzy, feather-headed aunt, who at forty-five still thinks she's a cheerleader.

GINGER. That's not a nice way to talk about my sister.

WINNIE. Well, from what everybody tells me, the only sport that interested her was backseat bingo.

GINGER. People who live in glass houses . . .

WINNIE. Dad says she was the graffiti queen of the fifties. "Phone Joan" was the password. "In the zone, phone Joan" . . . "Want your corn poned, phone Joan."

GINGER. He's just bitter because he went off to school and she didn't sit around and wait for four years.

WINNIE. He says she didn't wait fifteen minutes.

GINGER. Let's not get involved in semantics.

WINNIE. Semantics?!

GINGER. Yes. Joan started to date sometime between fifteen minutes *or* four years after he left. What difference does it make twenty-eight years later?

WINNIE. I'm a medical student who plans to become a psychiatrist. And I'd like to find the truth.

GINGER. Analyze! What else is a mother for?

WINNIE. So, Dad broke off with your nympho sister and took up with you. (*Winnie starts to sort and stack magazines.*)

GINGER. Your father and I had a great many interests in common.

WINNIE. You certainly did. You played high-school football together.

GINGER. Only one season.

WINNIE. Then eventually you two ass-patting football players got married.

GINGER. What exactly is your point?

WINNIE. Doesn't it seem a little freaky to you that Dad went to an all boys school, gave up your sister who loved sex, married a fellow football player and named his first daughter Eddie?

GINGER. Yes, that does seem a little freaky.

WINNIE. Why does he buy *Playgirl?* (*Winnie holds up that magazine.*)

GINGER. (*Shrugs.*) To look at the pictures.

WINNIE. That makes Dad even more suspect. (*Winnie starts for the kitchen.*)

GINGER. What are you so edgy about?

7

WINNIE. (*Turns.*) I don't know—I've been like this for two days.

GINGER. It's not like you . . . you're always so calm and logical.

WINNIE. I know. I've got screaming nerve ends. I feel if I don't keep physically busy, I'll have a breakdown.

GINGER. Maybe you should see a doctor.

WINNIE. No . . . I'll be all right. (*Offstage the front door slams.*)

EDDIE. (*Offstage.*) I'm home.

WINNIE. Excuse me . . . (*Winnie exits to the kitchen as Eddie Davis, husband and father of the household, appears in the arch* C. *He's an attractive man in his forties. He is dressed in rather chic khaki work suit. The costume of a county engineer.*)

EDDIE. Hi darling, how are you?

GINGER. Why didn't you marry my sister?

EDDIE. I didn't like her. I still don't. But if you want me to marry your sister, I'll do it. I'd do anything for you.

GINGER. Was she too sexy for you?

EDDIE. (*Nods.*) With too many people. But that doesn't matter. I'll go right over to her house now and tell her to get a divorce, so that we can get married, if that will make you happy.

GINGER. Why do you read *Playgirl?*

EDDIE. I'm a comparative shopper.

GINGER. Did you marry me because I was a football player?

EDDIE. Absolutely. And it's fun coming home to a tight end. But having known your sister, I would hardly have called that a genetic condition.

GINGER. I don't want to spend any more time talking about my sister's sexual preferences.

EDDIE. Neither do I. I'm what is known as a reconstructional engineer of hydraulic supervision. I spend my whole day filling potholes, why should I have to come home and talk about your sister? (*Winnie re-enters from the kitchen. She carries a spray bottle of furniture polish and a cloth.*)

GINGER. That's enough, Eddie.

EDDIE. I don't think it's enough at all. Just because you're a child psychologist who teaches at the high school level, how dare you have the temerity to question my sense of morality? I come home after work and I'm savagely attacked by the only person in the world who ever promised to love, honor and cherish me, because I'm not having sex with her sister. It's nothing I've given any thought to, so I have no defense, except to say I don't like belonging to large clubs.

8

WINNIE. I think Mom suspects you're gay.

EDDIE. That's only because the new morality has rendered most men my age impotent. We were public *machos* and closet Victorians who couldn't adjust to sexual liberation. (*Winnie sprays the drum table.*) Would you mind not spraying that aerosol pollutant all over me? If I want to be waxed, I'll go to a car wash. (*Winnie moves a few steps away.*) Whoever dreamed that the sweet, frightened, pristine girl you were originally afraid to kiss, would be grabbing you every night, twenty years later and screaming, "Perform, perform, perform!"

GINGER. (*Laughs.*) I'm only trying to make you forget your headaches.

WINNIE. Daddy, you can't be opposed to women's lib.

EDDIE. I'm not. But we grew up in a different sexual climate than you. Did your mother ever tell you about the first time we went to bed together?

WINNIE. (*Tight.*) No.

GINGER. I was a virgin.

WINNIE. I don't want to hear about it.

EDDIE. Why not?

WINNIE. I . . . just think . . . there are some things that shouldn't be talked about.

EDDIE. Hypocrites! All young people are hypocrites . . . You want to flaunt your free sex style but you don't want to hear that your parents ever went to bed together.

WINNIE. No . . . it's not that.

EDDIE. It was in a hotel room, in New York.

GINGER. On our honeymoon.

WINNIE. Oh, you mean you were married.

GINGER. That day.

EDDIE. Does that make it all right for you?

WINNIE. I'm sorry . . . I guess I'm a closet prude.

GINGER. Anyway, it was very romantic . . . your father sat on the edge of the bed, held my hand, and read to me for three hours.

EDDIE. Two hours.

WINNIE. You sat and read for three hours on your wedding night?

EDDIE. Two hours.

WINNIE.. Wow, what a trip! You held Mom's hand and read poetry?

9

GINGER. Sort of . . . The book was called, "All The Things You Should Know and *Don't.*"

WINNIE. (*Laughs.*) What?!

EDDIE. Please don't remind me of my debauched years.

WINNIE. What do you mean debauched?!

EDDIE. Any young man who doesn't know what to do on his honeymoon has had a debauched life. Neither one of us understood the medical terms, I'd have been better off with a copy of *Popular Mechanics.*

GINGER. You're going to have a coronary.

EDDIE. If it's free, I'll take it. In this economy it's the only kind of vacation this family can afford.

WINNIE. Things will get better.

EDDIE. They won't get better, the whole nation is standing on the brink of the French Revolution and nobody knows the lyrics of the "Marseillaise." The incumbents are the Royalists, the opposition are the Girondists, and the people are the Jacobins. Two hundred million people are waiting to storm the Bastille and the queen is shouting: "Get your peanuts roasted!" (*Winnie sprays the magazine rack.*)

WINNIE. Would you like some free analysis?

EDDIE. If you don't stop spraying me, they're going to come and haul me off to a wax museum! Are you really my daughter or some insane medical student in search of cadavers?

WINNIE. When I become a doctor, I'll pay you house calls.

EDDIE. Will I be able to afford them?

WINNIE. We'll cross that bridge when we get to it.

EDDIE. Winnie, you've never done a day's work in your life. You've never earned a dollar. But now you're twenty-one years old and I think you should know the truth . . . from the time you entered work and play school at the age of four, through kindergarten at six, until you become a psychiatrist at around fifty, I will have spent approximately four million dollars on your education, which does not include food, lodging, a car, and the two thousand dollars you spend on clothes every week. But I'm a parent and I expect neither credit nor gratitude, which I know you have no intention of giving. However, I would never have been able to do it if your mother had not been a successful prostitute.

WINNIE. (*Smiles.*) Sometimes I think you're a little kinky.

EDDIE. Don't try to bait me with your maudlin sentiment. I grew up during the Eisenhower administration when I was taught that father-knows-best. And I believed it. But by the time I got married and had children, along came a crazed doctor who convinced everybody men were pigs, women were equals and kids were kings. I was born into a whole lost tribe of men who've been tyrannized, at both ends of the generation gap.

GINGER. Your father was a wonderful man.

EDDIE. He hated me.

GINGER. Well, you can't really hold that against him. Nobody liked you very much.

EDDIE. You liked me.

GINGER. Not really.

EDDIE. Why did you marry me?

GINGER. I thought I could bring out your redeeming qualities.

EDDIE. In retrospect, how do you think you made out?

GINGER. Naturally, I failed, you didn't have any.

EDDIE. Thank you.

GINGER. But I still don't feel I've lost. And, incidentally, I don't believe there's that much difference between our generation and this generation.

EDDIE. You don't . . .

GINGER. No.

WINNIE. I'm going in and clean the kitchen. (*Winnie starts for the kitchen.*)

GINGER. Are you expecting company?

WINNIE. No.

EDDIE. I hope you haven't decided to sell the house.

WINNIE. I just have an urge to clean, is there anything wrong with that?

EDDIE. No, but it does come as a shocking departure from your natural instincts. (*Winnie turns at the door.*)

WINNIE. Not as shocking as some other departures you might be hearing about. (*Winnie exits to the kitchen.*)

EDDIE. What do you suppose that meant?

GINGER. I think it was simply an abstract answer to your somewhat rude, unsolicited comment on her sense of industry.

EDDIE. I know today's young people better than you, and I promise you, every seemingly abstract remark comes home to roost, fraught with meaning.

GINGER. Why don't you relax, pothole person, you're always trying to create problems where none exist.

11

EDDIE. All I can tell you, Virginia Carol Davis, is, if I'd been allowed to bring up my children the way your father brought up his, I wouldn't have to be concerned about remarks like that.

GINGER. My father was a very liberal parent.

EDDIE. But strict.

GINGER. No . . . not really . . . maybe more structured than we are . . .

EDDIE. *Structured?!* Your father and mother brought up three daughters and never had this conversation.

GINGER. They didn't have to, as far as I was concerned.

EDDIE. Oh, I *know!* But I remember when you were eighteen and I was *twenty-two,* your father said, "*Eddie,* I want her back here at midnight and in *one piece.*" Then right after I stood at attention and saluted, he put down his shotgun and frisked me for contraceptives. And I wore an American crew-cut! (*Ginger laughs.*) And you think there's no attitudinal difference between your generation and your daughter's.

GINGER. Not really. My mother, my daughter and I, *all women,* were obviously thinking the same thing sexually at about the same age.

EDDIE. Why didn't you say something?

GINGER. (*Shrugs.*) Why didn't you *do* something?

EDDIE. Fear. When Winnie was fifteen, I was instructed to say to her dates, "Here's her pills, bring her back by next Thursday." And you thought I was being overbearing and restrictive.

GINGER. No . . . But I didn't feel she should be deprived of her right to sexual freedom, the way I was . . . if that's what she *chose.*

EDDIE. And that's what she chose.

GINGER. So?

EDDIE. So I've got a twenty-one-year-old daughter, who's never worked a day in her life, and she's the sexual lioness of the hot pillow set.

GINGER. She's only had sex with one man.

EDDIE. For *three years,* four times a day, ten days a week! What are we talking about?

GINGER. They're in love.

EDDIE. You must be insane from playing football with boys. You got slapped on the helmet too many times! You've lost one of your building blocks. This could easily be the most bizarre discussion two tall people ever had. It's a drunken conversation between two strangers, in a bar, being held by a married couple in a living room, who aren't drinking.

GINGER. Do you want to rant or talk?

EDDIE. Rant! They're not in love with each other . . . they're simply two young sex maniacs who have discovered the best of all possible welfare states. She lives here with us, he lives with his parents, and I pay for the motel rooms on my daughter's dirty weekends.

GINGER. Sam is a very serious musician.

EDDIE. I don't want to hear about his neurosis, why doesn't he go out and get a job? I've never heard of two young people who have the hots for each other, not wanting to be together. Since they're free of all conventions, why don't they take a place of their own?

GINGER. Because Winnie feels that economic pressures might destroy what they have.

EDDIE. I've got a daughter who's gone through the looking glass! I'm the unwilling father of Alice in Wonderland. You're the lovable Queen of Hearts and I'm the Mad Hatter . . . (*Eddie jumps around the room.*) Hippety-hop! Hippety-hop! (*Eddie stops and turns to Ginger.*) What are we talking about?! I'm not asking if they ever expect to get married; all I want to know is, do they ever intend to live together? Is that too much for a father to ask?

GINGER. They probably do.

EDDIE. When?

GINGER. I have no idea.

EDDIE. Why don't you ask?

GINGER. Do you know what's wrong with you?

EDDIE. Yes, I'm sane. It's a terrible drawback for a parent in this day and age. I'm not an old-fashioned father who's concerned about what Sam's intentions are toward my daughter. Whatever he intended he's already *done*. I don't expect him to come to me and say, "Eddie, may I have your daughter's hand in marriage?" after he's had every other part of her from stem to stern. I just don't want him to scuttle her, and wave bon voyage from the iceberg.

GINGER. I don't even know what that means.

EDDIE. Neither do I because we're not nautical. But all I would like to know is, sometime in the distant future, when I'm an old hulk of a human being, and they do get married, are they still both going to live at home? Is my tombstone going to read: "Did they ever move in together?" That's what's wrong with me.

GINGER. No, that's not what's wrong with you.

EDDIE. What's wrong with me?

GINGER. In this situation, you're the victim of emotional frustration. You can't stand the fact that she's happy, he's happy and you're not.

EDDIE. My answer to that is, "Life's not always fair." Which makes about as much sense. But what would make me a bit more glad, not *happy*, just glad is, if she would move in with *his* family.

GINGER. It wouldn't work, because then he'd be happy, you'd be happy, but she'd be *unglad*.

EDDIE. Suppose we had Sam move in here?

GINGER. No. Because then he'd be happy, you'd be happy and I'd be miserable.

EDDIE. How come you'd be miserable?

GINGER. I am not going to have my *unmarried* daughter living in my home with a strange man.

EDDIE. How strange is he? We've known him since he was born. The first time I heard he was having an affair with my daughter, I told you he was a degenerate.

GINGER. What you'd like to do is break up their relationship.

EDDIE. No, you don't understand . . . I'm only trying to get them together. Who knows, maybe they'll get to like each other. They'll decide they can't live without each other and we'll throw them out. Let's move them in! They'll have no place else to go!

GINGER. Not under my roof.

EDDIE. Why not?

GINGER. People talk.

EDDIE. Don't you think they talk now?

GINGER. Only behind my back.

EDDIE. You mean that you don't care where, when or how often Sam and your daughter screw, as long as you can pretend you don't know about it.

GINGER. No, my darling Vulgarian . . . what I'm saying is, I am totally aware of their most personal relationship, and I have no objection to it. In fact, I approve; because I believe in sexual freedom for young people.

EDDIE. Besides, it keeps them off the streets. How many people get mugged in the back seat of a car? "It's ten o'clock . . . do you know where your children are?" I certainly do. She's at the nearest drive-in, lying down in the back of a Volkswagen camper, listening to a movie. But she'll be home by midnight because she's a good

14

girl, and I think I might go insane! Tell me, if you're such an advocate of sexual freedom, why won't you let them practice their favorite indoor sport here?

GINGER. Because I'd consider that immoral.

EDDIE. Darling . . . I think the time has come for you and me to say goodbye. We are not destined to be together very much longer because, one day, not far from now, men are going to appear with wet sheets and take one, or the other of us away. If it's soon, it will be you . . . if some times passes, I'm certain it will be me, and it all has to do with your logic. (*Eddie crosses and kisses Ginger.*) Goodbye. (*He starts* u.)

GINGER. Where are you going?

EDDIE. Around the bend! (*Eddie turns back to Ginger.*) Do you think when I stand here and listen to this conversation, I dance around and shout, "Einstein, Einstein, I'm married to Albert Einstein," just because I don't understand one word you say?! You're a champion-at-large for sexual freedom who thinks it's personally immoral! . . . That's like saying you don't believe in smoking, but you think the government should subsidize the tobacco industry!

GINGER. You know *exactly* what I'm trying to say.

EDDIE. If you are trying to say, exactly what I think you're trying to say, I'm going to have you arrested for fraud. (*The phone rings.*)

GINGER. What I mean is that I believe all young people should have an unrepressed, healthy sex life. But not in my house. (*The phone rings a second time; Ginger crosses* u. *to answer it.*)

EDDIE. You seem to feel the same way about middle-aged people in your house.

GINGER. Kiss it, baby, I can still touch my toes. (*She picks up the phone.*) Hello . . . just a minute, Sam.

EDDIE. That remark is the penultimate in nepotism. (*Ginger opens the swinging door to the kitchen.*)

GINGER. It's Sam, for you. (*Ginger shrugs and crosses back* c. *to hang up the phone.*) And, incidentally, I feel the same way about old people, and sex, as I do about young people and sex.

EDDIE. Put it down on your list of health aids for senior citizens. (*Ginger hangs up the phone.*) All I can tell you is, sexual freedom is one of the prime causes of America's economic skid. There was a time, in this great nation, when a man who didn't want to get laid at home, went out, got a hooker, paid his money and took his choice. No more! Prostitution is a dying art. The American girl-child is on the pill before she's off the bottle. They're taught to screw from the cradle to the grave. They've destroyed the free enterprise system by putting prostitution out of business. There are more hookers on welfare today than there are Eskimoes in Alaska. Bring back Victorian morality and we'll be rid of the welfare state. I'll vote for any man who extolls the platform of "Peace and Prosperity through Prostitution."

GINGER. As soon as Winnie gets off the phone, I'll call the doctor.

EDDIE. No, no, I think I solved the whole problem about why young people don't co-habitate ·anymore . . . it's not malice . . . it's lack of recognition. They spend so much time naked in bed, that when they meet socially, they don't recognize each other. It's a generation that's discovered an entire reverse twist, they disguise themselves in nudity.

GINGER. How many convolutions a minute does it take, for your warped mind to function. (*Offstage the door slams with such force it seems to rock the house.*)

EDDIE. The animal is loose! (*Tinker Davis, the sixteen-year-old son of the Davis clan, appears in the arch c. Tinker is perhaps the most handsome, energy-packed, volatile young man ever created. He is, at best, a wild, off-the-wall original, who is totally free and uninhibited. As a consequence, the next few lines are done in rapid succession at high decibel rate.*)

TINKER. I think all women are *weird!*

GINGER. Don't retract that statement because I'm here!

TINKER. I wasn't going to!

GINGER. I didn't think so.

EDDIE. What's wrong with Billie today?

TINKER. She always wants me to do what I don't want to do, to keep me from doing what I do want to do, because she wants me to do what I don't want to do with her, instead of doing what I do want to.

GINGER. Tink, why don't you go up to your room, open the window and fly south!

TINKER. You know, Mom, you're a very neurotic lady.

GINGER. You're right. And I seem to be getting more neurotic all the time. But at least I know why. It's because I keep having this kind of conversation with you and your father, about the girl next door and your sister, and I wonder when, if ever, either or both of you, are going to grow up. That's what's making me so neurotic.

TINKER. Stay loose, Mom, and stop worrying. (*Tinker heads for the stairs.*) You see, it's much easier to deal with men, then women,

16

sexually, 'cause you can always be sure what they want. Stop being so uptight.

EDDIE. He's right, Virginia, *relax.*

TINKER. You see, Dad understands.

EDDIE. *Of course.* He's a young stud and he's just high spirited.

TINKER. That's right. I'm feeling my way, I'm experimenting.

EDDIE. And I think we agree he should be allowed the same sexual freedom his sister has.

GINGER. There must be a pothole here somewhere.

EDDIE. (*Laughs.*) No, no . . . come on . . .

TINKER. I'm almost seventeen years old and curious. Is there anything wrong with that?

EDDIE. No, every normal, healthy boy is curious at sixteen.

GINGER. What happened to you?

EDDIE. I was curious . . . and frightened.

GINGER. Do you have a different excuse now?

EDDIE. No, the same.

GINGER. Great . . . now, Tink, what are you *really* trying to tell us?

TINKER. Nothing. Just that I've reached a very exciting, uncertain age and I haven't made up my mind yet.

GINGER. *Sexually.*

TINKER. That's right.

GINGER. (*To Eddie.*) Your witness.

EDDIE. What do you mean?

TINKER. That I'm curious, uncertain and I'd like to experiment.

EDDIE. With what?

TINKER. With *sex*, Dad.

EDDIE. What kind of . . . curious, uncertain experiments do you have in mind?

TINKER. That's what I haven't decided yet.

EDDIE. Do I understand that means you intend to experiment with everything?

TINKER. Of course.

GINGER. What your father means is . . .

TINKER. I know what he means and I don't like labels. Let's just say I intend to satisfy my curiosity.

EDDIE. With *everybody?*

TINKER. Well, I don't want to be so provincial that I get tied down to one sex this early in life, and discover later I've made a terrible mistake.

EDDIE. Oh, sure. But since you said you haven't really decided

17

yet . . . maybe you should postpone the whole experiment just . . . until, after you've married and have children or . . . or, whichever comes first. How about that?

TINKER. You know the difference between you and Mom? She's uptight 'til she knows the problem, then she becomes completely supportive. You're always completely supportive until you know the problem, then you get uptight.

EDDIE. Yes, well, I had a very eerie childhood. The whole structure was only men and women, it was weird! Forgive me, I sometimes have trouble relating to the real, normal world of today. My strange upbringing has given me many distorted views of life; whereas, your mother, who played football with boys, has a much more healthy view of the problems that exist in bedlam.

TINKER. But certainly even with your background, you're liberated enough to know there's nothing wrong with sex, as long as both partners are people.

EDDIE. My darling son, or whatever you decide to be, I believe *that* as surely as I know the world is flat. And even if you decide to enter a sexual bestiary, I will somehow make the adjustment. But if I don't, your mother will, and after your wedding, all three of you can come and dance on my grave. But let me give you one last piece of advice . . . don't ever lie down with a gorilla, until after he's told you he loves you. (*Tinker starts up the stairs and turns.*)

TINKER. Isn't life exciting? I'm going up and take a long, hot tub, then I must lie down and rest, because tonight I'm going to McDonald's, and then to hell! (*Tinker laughs and exits.*)

EDDIE. As soon as whatever it is comes to pick you up, I'll rattle your cage. (*Ginger turns to her husband.*)

GINGER. Well, you said he was high spirited and he said he was curious. I didn't know what you both meant then, but certainly I do now!

EDDIE. Hold me in your arms, and tell me once more, how happy my children are going to make me.

GINGER. I said, in your *old* age.

EDDIE. *This is* my old age! And what have I got? A daughter who's an unpaid hooker and a son who's planning to become the unknown fag! And I promise you, he's the one who'll get married, and I'll be the father of the bride. We'll have a big, expensive church wedding. He and I will march down the aisle, the music will play . . . dum . . . dum . . . da . . . de . . . da . . . dum . . . dum . . . (*Eddie marches in cadence to "Lohengrin" and sings.*) And when I give him away, *you'll cry!*

GINGER. Maybe we'll like the boy.

EDDIE. We're living out the last days of Sodom and you're saying "please pass the salt." We won't like the boy! In six months they'll be divorced and he won't even get alimony. He'll come back and live with us for the rest of his life. Who appointed me Pied Piper?!

GINGER. All right, settle down.

EDDIE. To what?

GINGER. The problem of your son?

EDDIE. Why do you think he's a problem, dear lady? He's a blessing, and a joy.

GINGER. What would you like to do about him?

EDDIE. Seriously?

GINGER. Of course, *seriously*.

EDDIE. Kill him! Go out in the street and get some stones, we'll have a Biblical Baccanal. I'll invite our friends to the barbecue.

GINGER. Will you please calm down.

EDDIE. There's nothing to calm down about! The bomb has dropped and he's the only survivor, don't you understand that?

GINGER. Well, I think you're wrong.

EDDIE. All right, what shall we do?

GINGER. I think this is a situation where we should take a very strong, united stand and adjust to his problem. (*Eddie takes a long beat, as he regards Ginger.*)

EDDIE. Under the circumstances, don't you feel that's a little too cruel?

GINGER. In what way?

EDDIE. To burden him with so much kindness, in his moment of indecision.

GINGER. I'm not sure you understood what Tinker meant.

EDDIE. Oh, I think I did.

GINGER. He said he was un*cer*tain and *cur*ious.

EDDIE. Yes. but he was un*cer*tain about girls and *cur*ious about boys.

GINGER. I don't think that's what he meant.

EDDIE. He also said he planned to ex*per*iment.

GINGER. Maybe he meant with girls.

EDDIE. No. I think he's already done that experiment.

GINGER. You're not serious!

EDDIE. Oh, yes, I am.

GINGER. You mean he's done *it*, with that darling Billie next door?

EDDIE. That would be my guess.

GINGER. That's terrible!

EDDIE. Well, given a choice, wouldn't you prefer Billie was pregnant and he wasn't?

GINGER. Do you mean if I had to decide between Billie and some tacky boy we don't even know?

EDDIE. Somehow, I think we've lost the whole problem.

GINGER. Well, I'm absolutely outraged! How dare he do *it* with that gorgeous child?!

EDDIE. I wish you'd stop calling it, *"it."*

GINGER. Well, now I'm really furious! How could she allow herself to be *molested* by some dirty, old homosexual.

EDDIE. That's your *son* you're talking about.

GINGER. I don't care, she's a girl.

EDDIE. (*Shrugs.*) He is, too.

GINGER. And if this situation is not a product of your warped mind, to rationalize his neurotic behavior, then what can he possibly do with a boy that he can't do with her?

EDDIE. Reverse the question and I'll answer it.

GINGER. (*Thinks.*) What can a boy possibly do with him that she can't?

EDDIE. Exactly.

GINGER. (*A long beat.*) Oh . . . I'm becoming a great deal less supportive. But why would he do *it* to that fresh, beautiful child?

EDDIE. It's traditional.

GINGER. Then he should be made to marry her?

EDDIE. You've become an insane feminist right before my entire eyes. They can't get married.

GINGER. I'd like to know why not!

EDDIE. They're both sixteen years old!

GINGER. But in ten years they'll both be twenty-six.

EDDIE. You've become magnificently irrational.

GINGER. No! If they're old enough to have sex, they're old enough to get married.

EDDIE. How come you don't feel that way about your daughter?

GINGER. She's over age! She's allowed to do anything she wants to do. I have no jurisdiction over that relationship, but I do over this one. Call him down here, I want you to talk to him.

EDDIE. I never want to talk to him again, as long as he lives.

GINGER. Then I'll talk to him.

EDDIE. About what? He told you he was curious and planned on experimenting.

20

GINGER. It's too late for him to be curious or to experiment. He's practically a father!

EDDIE. God forbid!

GINGER. Oh, there goes Mr. Macho, it's all right for your daughter to be a sex object, but *God forbid* your son should be trapped by a mere *girl*.

EDDIE. That's not what I meant, at all. I don't think it's all right for my daughter to be a sex object, and what I mean was God forbid my son should become a father. It could end civilization as we know it! The whole concept is staggering. It's like Caligula with a family! (*Winnie enters, very quietly, from the kitchen. She's very subdued. She says softly:*)

WINNIE. Mom . . . (*Her mother and father turn to her and her tone changes the tenor of the scene.*) Sam just called.

GINGER. I know. (*Winnie moves to her father.*)

WINNIE. Dad . . . I love you very much. (*Eddie is somewhat taken aback by the sudden softness of his daughter.*)

EDDIE. I love you, too, baby.

WINNIE. You're a wonderful father.

EDDIE. Well, maybe . . . and maybe not. (*Eddie reaches up and touches his daughter's hair.*)

WINNIE. And now you're going to have one of your wishes come true. I'm moving out.

EDDIE. When?

WINNIE. Soon.

GINGER. Where are you going to move?

WINNIE. I'll find a flat here in town. (*Eddie now becomes the complete father.*)

EDDIE. Wait . . . wait . . . just a minute. How do you expect to live?

WINNIE. I'll get a sales job, or work as a secretary.

EDDIE. No, no . . . forget it, you're not moving out.

GINGER. Just a minute, Eddie . . .

EDDIE. (*Eddie on top.*) There is no just a minute; she's not leaving, I will not have her living alone in a flat! It's too dangerous . . . *that's it!*

WINNIE. But I won't really be alone . . .

GINGER. (*To Eddie.*) Besides, you're the one who said . . .

EDDIE. Never mind what I *said*, this is reality!

WINNIE. Daddy, let's be a little calm and logical.

EDDIE. (*Yells.*) I *am* calm! (*Tinker comes bouncing down the stairs.*) And I intend to be logical.

21

TINKER. Hello, sister . . . my God, you look exactly like Halloween!

EDDIE. What are you doing here?!

TINKER. I'm going to get some lettuce leaves to soothe my eyes.

EDDIE. You are not wasting my lettuce leaves on your eyes, they're too expensive to even eat!

TINKER. How do you feel about tea bags?

EDDIE. You just sit down and shut up, or I'll have you arrested as a child molester! (*Eddie turns to the other people.*) And I don't care about fem-lib or sexual freedom . . . I'm the head of this house, so you're going to listen to me and do what I say.

TINKER. My father, the dictator.

EDDIE. You can't just move out of here into a flat, and take a job.

WINNIE. Why not?

EDDIE. Because it will reflect on me. People will think I put you out.

WINNIE. (*Smiles.*) No, they won't, at all.

EDDIE. But what about your education? You can't give up medicine now.

WINNIE. Oh, no . . . I intend to go back to school.

EDDIE. Then why move out, at all?

WINNIE. Because I have to, Daddy.

EDDIE. Is this crazy Sam's idea?

WINNIE. I don't want you to blame Sam.

EDDIE. I won't blame him. I'll kill him!

GINGER. Wait just a minute . . . did Sam ask you to marry him!

WINNIE. The rabbit died.

GINGER. How marvelous.

TINKER. You mean you're pregnant?

WINNIE. That's right.

EDDIE. The rabbit died?! (*Winnie nods.*)

TINKER. After all this time you should have it stuffed and mounted.

EDDIE. (*To Tinker.*) You're not even supposed to know about those things, you sex maniac! When I was your age, I didn't even know why rabbits multiplied!

GINGER. How did you happen to get pregnant?

TINKER. Oh, *come on,* Mom.

WINNIE. I stopped taking the pill.

GINGER. Why?

WINNIE. For the same reason any woman stops.

TINKER. To trap the guy!

WINNIE. No, Tink, you're wrong. I just wanted to have a baby. (*Ginger hugs her daughter.*)

GINGER. Oh, darling, I'm so happy for you.

WINNIE. Thanks, Mom. Now you know why I'm moving out.

EDDIE. My God, I'm going to be a grandfather.

TINKER. I wish I knew what I was going to be.

EDDIE. Dead.

WINNIE. (*Smiles.*) I guess that's why I've been so edgy lately. Now, if you don't mind, I'll go up and lie down. (*Winnie moves to the stairs and turns.*) It's something I've wanted so badly. I'm happy and tired, all at the same time. (*Winnie smiles and exits up the stairs.*)

GINGER. (*To Eddie.*) Well . . . there goes your little girl.

EDDIE. Oh, sure. (*Eddie stands a long quiet beat.*) I wish she'd become a doctor first.

GINGER. What difference would that have made?

EDDIE. She could have delivered her own child.

GINGER. (*Smiles.*) You're terrible.

TINKER. Well, from my point of view it's a drag.

GINGER. Why, Uncle Tink?

TINKER. I could never spend the rest of my life with one man. (*Ginger and Eddie stare at Tinker.*)

GINGER. Get him out of the room!!

EDDIE. Get out of the room! (*Tinker goes to the stairs and turns.*)

TINKER. All right. So I won't look stunning tonight at McDonalds. (*And Tinker exits.*)

EDDIE. (*Calls.*) Oh, you'll look stunning all right, because by that time you'll be embalmed! (*Eddie turns back to Ginger.*)

GINGER. Well . . .

EDDIE. She's moving out of the house.

GINGER. See, if you just wish hard enough for something, you get it, and when you get it, you don't always want it.

EDDIE. I guess I must feel like your father did. Your first child leaves to get married, and the house is never the same.

GINGER. Worse than that . . . after she's gone, whenever we go up and look at her room, it will be clean.

EDDIE. You know, I just can't imagine her being married and living alone with Sam.

GINGER. (*Laughs.*) She can.

EDDIE. No, no. You know I'm crazy for Sam. He's young and quiet and carries a low profile.

GINGER. That might be a nice change for her.

EDDIE. But he's dreary, nothing seems to excite him. He's the only human being I've ever known who has no personality at all . . . none . . . none . . . if life is a song, Sam is a hum. I can't imagine how he got her pregnant.

GINGER. Oh, I can. That process doesn't take a lot of noise or athletic ability. During our college courtship, do you remember how many sporting events we sat through, in the wind, and the rain, and the snow and the sleet, cheering on the home team? Then going out to the club with the gang and reliving every play.

EDDIE. (*Smiles.*) Yep. And that's what Winnie's been deprived of.

GINGER. That's right. She's been deprived of absolute *boredom!*

EDDIE. Boredom?

GINGER. Utter! I learned all about hockey and soccer and spent my formative years muttering, "There must be another game in town." Through the long, dreary winters I was taught that a woman's place was in the kitchen, and a man's place was in front of the television set. And at the same age, my daughter learned that a woman's place was in love, and that she could also be a doctor. Now that's what I call liberation.

EDDIE. I always thought you loved sports.

GINGER. I did. I had a warped sense of equality.

EDDIE. Is that the reason you took the television set out of our bedroom?

GINGER. Eddie . . . we were married for three years before I got pregnant.

EDDIE. What about your first high school sweetheart, Tommy Green. He was very quiet.

GINGER. (*Smiles. A long beat.*) He certainly was. (*Eddie watches ginger, puzzled.*)

EDDIE. What does that mean?

GINGER. I'll never tell. But . . . (*Smiles.*) he always said I competed with boys on the wrong level. I used my athletic prowess, instead of my brain prowess.

EDDIE. Whereas; your daughter found an entire third prowess, sex.

GINGER. Well, I'd better start making out a wedding list.

EDDIE. Before the blessed event.

GINGER. You know, maybe the house wouldn't be so lonely, if you hadn't talked so much.

EDDIE. Funny you should say that, because you know what I've been thinking?

GINGER. Yes, and the answer is no.

24

EDDIE. I haven't asked the question yet.

GINGER. They are not coming here to live with us, after they're married.

EDDIE. I don't know why not. It might be fun to have them here, at least till the baby is born.

GINGER. Cut her loose, Father Davis, she's another man's girl now.

EDDIE. Oh, I wasn't trying to hold on to her.

GINGER. Of course you weren't.

EDDIE. I just thought she'd be more comfortable here, in familiar surroundings.

GINGER. Newlywed girls don't want familiar of *filial* surroundings.

EDDIE. But it might be better for them, economically.

GINGER. Let's put it in this perspective: how would you have liked to have moved in here, with *my* mother and father, after we were married?

EDDIE. Well, that's different . . . your mother and father were so Victorian, we'd have felt restricted. We couldn't really have . . . pulled out all the stops.

GINGER. (*Nods.*) So we got our own apartment, and didn't anyway.

EDDIE. What are you talking about?

GINGER. Oh, come on, for the first five years we were married, I thought you were a missionary . . . you kept saying, "Be my savage!" . . . But I was afraid if I moved you'd stick me in a pot of boiling water.

EDDIE. That's a terrible thing to say.

GINGER. Truth is one of life's great equalizers, that's why most women lie to their men.

EDDIE. I taught you the art of love.

GINGER. Yes, that's what most husbands think. But actually sex is only a natural craft, it can be learned anywhere. It's like dancing or tandem-biking, one can even do it alone, but it's much more pleasant with a partner . . . *sometimes.* And once you've learned it, you not only never forget how to do it, but if you really practice it, and perfect the fine points, everybody wants to dance with you.

EDDIE. What kind of conversation is this?!

GINGER. It's the kind of conversation that's been looking for a place to happen. And this is the place. Your daughter and future son-in-law, are not coming here to live.

EDDIE. I just thought . . .

GINGER. No. That's the last word.

EDDIE. You mean . . . you're turning her out?

GINGER. I'm turning her loose . . . she's getting married and having a child . . . it won't be long before Tinker is gone . . . I think the time has almost come for you and me to move on.

EDDIE. You mean, leave the house . . . ?

GINGER. Why should Winnie and Sam live in a flat? They're starting a family.

EDDIE. What you're saying is . . . turn the house over to them.

GINGER. As soon as Tink goes away to school. Life and time move on, Eddie . . . it's what my parents did for us when Winnie was born . . . it's a new generation.

EDDIE. (*Wanders about.*) It won't be easy.

GINGER. No.

EDDIE. All of my youth . . . all my dreams and most of my love is in this house.

GINGER. I know.

EDDIE. And you're right . . . a girl shouldn't live with a terrible father.

GINGER. You're not a terrible father.

EDDIE. Yes. There are times I love her more than I love you.

GINGER. That's fair. I'm her, twenty years ago.

EDDIE. When I was captain of the football team, I never dreamed that one day I'd be married to a forty-three year old woman.

GINGER. I did.

EDDIE. I love you.

GINGER. And I love you. (*the curtain falls ending Scene 1.*)

ACT ONE

Scene 2

TIME: *Three hours later.*
SETTING: *The same.*
AT RISE: *The front door slams. Eddie appears in the arch c. crosses to the stairs and calls.*

EDDIE. Virginia! (*Eddie waits, Ginger comes out of the kitchen.*)

GINGER. Yes.

EDDIE. (*At stairs.*) Come down stairs.

GINGER. No. (*Eddie now realizes where Ginger is and turns toward the living room.*) Where have you been for the past two hours?

EDDIE. Downtown. Making arrangements.

GINGER. What for?

EDDIE. The *wedding*. I never realized what a responsibility it is to be a father of the bride.

GINGER. What arrangements have you wrought?

EDDIE. I booked the church . . .

GINGER. When?

EDDIE. A week from Sunday.

GINGER. Don't you think you should have consulted the participants first?

EDDIE. No, I don't believe in long arrangements before a wedding when the bride-to-be is pregnant and *my* daughter. I'd rather not have to help deliver the baby before either party says "I do."

GINGER. What else did you arrange?

EDDIE. I bought the flowers, rented the hotel ballroom, got the caterer, made appointments for blood test and bought the booze . . .

GINGER. My you've been busy.

EDDIE. Oh, sure . . . now where shall I book them for their honeymoon?

GINGER. In a Latin American maternity ward. (*The door bell rings.*)

EDDIE. You know, darling, you're very little help.

GINGER. I try to be . . . (*Ginger crosses U.*) I'll get it. (*Offstage the door slams.*) I guess I don't have to. (*In the archway, there appears Billie Grey, the girl next door. Billie is sixteen years old, and probably the most glorious female animal who ever lived. She is totally filled with fire; but it a predator, who is never involved with anger.*)

BILLIE. Hi!

GINGER. Hello, Billie.

BILLIE. Hello, Mr. Davis.

EDDIE. Hi, Billie . . .

BILLIE. Where is he?

GINGER. He's up in his room. (*Billie crosses to the stairs.*)

BILLIE. (*Calls.*) Babes!

TINKER. (*Offstage.*) Yeah!

BILLIE. Get down here! (*She turns to Ginger and Eddie.*) There are two or three things I want to tell you, and I don't want you to feel I'm being aggressive. Babes is *my* man . . .

27

EDDIE. Well . . .

BILLIE. No, not *"well,"* Mr. Davis . . . I love Babes. And if he wants to fulfill every carnal curiosity, it's going to be with *me;* which he has not done up till now. If he's going to experiment, it will be with me. I will take care of any sexual fantasy he has, but he is not going to McDonald's tonight.

EDDIE. Which I don't really feel is a sexual fantasy . . . or maybe I'm wrong . . . since over three billion people have enjoyed eating hamburgers, they're less interested in eating anything else.

GINGER. Eddie . . .

EDDIE. No darling, let's be honest, if one puts pickle and relish and catsup on anything, the American public will eat it and be totally happy. It could entirely change the sex habits of the complete American public.

GINGER. Eddie!

EDDIE. (*To Billie.*) You were saying . . .

BILLIE. Babes is also *not* going to play with the football team!

GINGER. Well, Billie, I don't think you can deprive him of his basic right to . . . (*There's a long beat.*)

EDDIE. The football team?

BILLIE. He went out for it this afternoon.

EDDIE. (*Yells.*) Get him down here!

GINGER. (*On top.*) Tink!

TINKER. (*Offstage.*) Yes, Mom . . .

EDDIE. Get down here!

GINGER. (*Quietly.*) Now, Eddie, let's reason with him.

BILLIE. *I'm* not going to reason with him.

GINGER. (*To Billie.*) There's no reason you should reason, you're emotionally involved.

EDDIE. What the hell am I?

GINGER. You're his *father.*

EDDIE. Ho . . . ho . . . ho . . . ho! (*Tinker appears on the staircase.*)

TINKER. Did you call me, Mom?

GINGER. Yes, I did. Your *father* wants to talk to you.

TINKER. I have the feeling that this is a very hostile room.

EDDIE. Sit down! (*Tinker crosses and sits.*) We have just received the stunning news that you reported for football practice today.

TINKER. That's right.

BILLIE. Why?!

TINKER. I have my reasons.

28

EDDIE. I'm sure you do and I don't mean to be arbitrary, nor am I vindictive, but in the light of a previous conversation I am going to say something to you that no father has ever said to a son before . . . *Tink* . . . you are not going to play football with boys.

TINKER. You're missing the point, Dad.

EDDIE. I doubt it . . .

TINKER. I don't care whether or not I *play* football. I just want to be on the team.

EDDIE. And that's exactly why you're not going to.

TINKER. Give me a good reason.

GINGER. It's a dangerous game, darling . . . football is a contact sport.

TINKER. I know.

BILLIE. No!

EDDIE. The answer is, *no!*

GINGER. You see, Tink . . . I played football against boys, and your father played football with boys . . . or whatever, and we have no serious objection to your wanting to enjoy yourself . . .

EDDIE. Depending upon the sport!

BILLIE. You might get badly hurt.

TINKER. In a locker room?!

BILLIE. Particularly in a locker room.

EDDIE. It's the maternal instinct, Billie doesn't want a fatherless child.

TINKER. (*To Billie.*) Did you tell them you were pregnant?

BILLIE. Of course not.

GINGER. More to the point, darling, *are* you pregnant?

BILLIE. (*Shocked.*) Of course not, Mrs. Davis, I'd never resort to that kind of dishonesty.

GINGER. Suddenly life seems simple.

EDDIE. Because that's that best piece of news we've had all day.

BILLIE. Babes, here's the bottom line . . . if you insist on going out for the team, I'm going to school tomorrow and tell everybody you're *straight!* (*Eddie and Ginger stare at each other in disbelief.*)

TINKER. You wouldn't dare!

BILLIE. I think we'd better go over to my house and communicate. (*Billie turns and exits. Tinker follows.*)

GINGER. (*Calls.*) Is your mother home? (*Offstage the front door slams.*) I don't think that's a good idea.

EDDIE. Oh, let them go; they've done everything else; and with a little bit of luck he may only turn out to be bi-sexual.

GINGER. But they're *children,* Eddie.

EDDIE. No, no, you don't understand, there are no more children. There are only old people and electric sex machines. They're programmed to be plugged in and turned on at fourteen, and run as long as that current lasts, then find a new machine.

GINGER. Well, what can we do about it?

EDDIE. Virginia, I have given that question a great deal of serious thought, and I've reached the conclusion that I don't know. Our children have *done* everything there is to be *done*. It's something we've asked each other all through our married life. We've stayed awake nights, we've discussed it, we've analyzed it, we've let it torture and torment us, and we've never found the answer because we've always had the wrong question.

GINGER. What's the right question?

EDDIE. The right question is . . . what can we undo about it? They've always *done* and then we've tried to *do*. But finally, after all these years, I've realized, you can't *do* a done.

GINGER. You mean you've got to undo a done.

EDDIE. Right!

GINGER. Then what are we going to undo about it?

EDDIE. I'm glad you asked that because the answer is simple. We are not going to undo *nothing*.

GINGER. Be serious, Eddie.

EDDIE. I am serious . . . it's all over, don't you understand? They'll make their mistakes and they'll survive the way we did, the way our parents did and the way their parents did. I'm sick of Gethsemane! So take my hand and we'll walk up the hill together. There are two crosses left . . .

GINGER. I refuse to accept that.

EDDIE. Because you're totally insane, you're lady crazy, why did I humor you all these years by telling you the earth was round?

GINGER. I believe that life has order.

EDDIE. That's totally fascistic point of view . . . and the reason I'm filling potholes.

GINGER. So I'm going on, write a list for Winnie's wedding and we'll deal with Tink's problem later.

EDDIE. I have a much more constructive idea . . . I would suggest you start turning the house into a fort; because when Billie's parents learn the truth about their daughter and your son, the vigilantes will swoop down and hang him from the highest goal post in town, and that's the closest he'll ever get to playing football!

GINGER. They wouldn't dare . . .

EDDIE. Billie's father is a ranking member of the F.B.I., and they also believe that life has order. (*Offstage the doorbell rings. Ginger and Eddie stand a long beat.*) I'm not going to get it. (*Ginger exits through the arch* C. *and off. Eddie wanders about the room.*)

GINGER. (*Offstage.*) Hello, Sam . . . come in . . . (*Eddie nods knowingly, at the thought of another crisis. Ginger reappears in the arch, followed by Sam Graham. Sam is a young man of twenty-two. He's attractive in an average way but his major character traits are that he seems shy, introverted, ill at ease and without opinion, in any given social situation.*) Sam's here, dear.

EDDIE. I'm sure he's not here to see me.

GINGER. I'll go get Winnie . . . (*Ginger turns and exits up the stairs. Sam and Eddie are left in the silence of the room. The young man shuffles uncomfortably.*)

SAM. Hello, Ed.

EDDIE. Hello, Sam.

SAM. I'm sure you're mad at me.

EDDIE. Why?

SAM. The rabbit died.

EDDIE. Well, I heard he'd been sick for a long time.

SAM. I'm sorry . . .

EDDIE. Why? That wasn't your fault, Sam . . . lots of rabbits die . . . why should I be concerned about one lousy rabbit? . . . I can always afford another rabbit.

SAM. You know what I mean.

EDDIE. No, I don't . . . you see, I don't care about the rabbit. I'm concerned that my daughter is pregnant!

SAM. Oh . . . oh . . . don't worry about that . . . I'm . . . I'm . . . I'm going to . . . I intend . . . to do . . . the right thing.

EDDIE. You don't seem too sure . . .

SAM. Oh, I'm sure.

EDDIE. (*Leers.*) So am I!

SAM. But I will admit that the thought is a little frightening.

EDDIE. (*Nods.*) Don't worry about it. As the years go on and you raise a family, you'll wish you could be a character in a Kafka play.

SAM. You're scaring me.

EDDIE. I wish somebody had scared me.

SAM. I still remember the first time I met Winnie . . . but I never thought it would end up this way.

EDDIE. Breaks of the game, Sam.

SAM. How did you meet your wife?

EDDIE. We never met. She's my karma.

SAM. Oh, that's terrifying.

EDDIE. (*Nods.*) Tell me, Sam, in all the years you've been having sex with Winnie, hadn't it ever occurred to you that this might happen?

SAM. No. (*Eddie stands and stares at Sam.*) You see, I had absolute faith in her.

EDDIE. (*Nods.*) It's a simple, maniacal male-failing. (*Ginger appears on the stairs.*)

GINGER. Winnie will be right down, *son*. (*Eddie and Sam turn toward the glowing Ginger who enters the room proper.*)

SAM. (*Shrugs.*) Thanks, Mom . . . did you hear the rabbit died?

GINGER. Yes, and my husband's arranged a marvelous funeral. He's rented the church, got the minister, selected the floral arrangements, one of which is an empty hutch, and he's bought the booze.

SAM. I don't drink.

GINGER. Would you like some coffee?

EDDIE. That's what we drink here . . . coffee . . . it keeps the heart pumping . . . stops coronary arrest . . . if I wasn't a big coffee drinker, I'd have been dead three times today.

SAM. What happened?

EDDIE. I found out my daughter was pregnant. The sixteen-year-old girl next door is consorting with my son. And he'd like to experiment with boys. But, I don't know what in hell I'll do if Tink's rabbit dies.

GINGER. Is this a father-son discussion?

EDDIE. No.

SAM. Oh, no—

EDDIE. No, no—I have a son . . . well, let's just say there's a boy in my life.

GINGER. Aren't there some questions you should ask Sam? . . . I mean the kind of questions Dad asked you?

EDDIE. Well . . . sure . . . but certainly, "What are your intentions?" is out. And about asking for her hand. He hasn't asked.

SAM. May I have her hand?

EDDIE. Or whatever comes first . . .

GINGER. How do you intend to support your wife . . . and child?

EDDIE. Easily. There are people all over the world playing Punk Rock, and making a fortune.

SAM. I don't play Punk Rock.

EDDIE. Intuitively, I knew that . . . you're into . . .

SAM. Symphony . . . percussion. At the moment, I have a gig with the local symphony. (*Eddie stands and nods, totally lost.*) I'm a boom-warmer.

EDDIE. (*Nods.*) Somehow, I suspected that.

SAM. (*Smiles.*) A boom-warmer is an apprentice percussionist . . . he taps gently on the huge gong to keep it warm for the lead percussionist, all through the symphony. But at the same time, he must make certain it can't be heard.

EDDIE. Not heard?

SAM. It's very tricky.

GINGER. Then why keep it warm?

SAM. Because if a percussionist hits a cold gong, it shatters.

EDDIE. Darling, have you ever been involved in gong banging?

GINGER. No, I never have.

EDDIE. You've just been lucky. (*Eddie turns to Sam.*) You mean, you keep the gong warm all night, then somebody else comes in and bangs it?!

SAM. That's right.

EDDIE. Somehow, that doesn't seem fair to me.

GINGER. Well, Darling, I hate to break this news to you, but there have always been the warmers and the bangers.

EDDIE. Tell me Sam, is there much of a future in your sort of work?

SAM. Well . . . if one works hard and sticks with symphony orchestras, I would say there's almost none. (*Eddie nods knowingly.*) But it's nothing to worry about, that's a sort of avocation.

GINGER. You mean you have a real vocation?

SAM. Yes . . . I'm writing a symphony.

EDDIE. I'm glad to hear that . . . for a moment there, I was worried about how you'd support your wife and child. But now, I realize you don't have to worry about that, I do.

SAM. No, no . . . it will all be taken care of, Winnie will get a job.

GINGER. *Winnie,* will get a job?

SAM. That's the essence of Fem-Lib . . .

EDDIE. You know, Sam, I must tell you something honestly. From the time you were born, I didn't like you. But now, I really loathe you . . . what are you, some sort of insane savage! This isn't the jungle where a man sends his wife out to hunt food . . . this is the cultured, sophisticated midwest.

SAM. Well, going out and working was Winnie's idea.

EDDIE. Don't you have any guts or spine?

GINGER. Eddie . . .

SAM. Yes, of course . . . I do exactly what Winnie wants. (*Winnie appears on the stairs. She is radiant, like the bride-mother.*)

WINNIE. Hello, Boom-Boom.

SAM. (*Turns.*) Hi . . . (*Winnie enters the room proper.*)

WINNIE. Don't worry about anything, Dad, it will be all taken care of.

EDDIE. All right, darling . . . but it seems to me that . . .

WINNIE. Daddy.

GINGER. Eddie . . . (*Eddie turns to Ginger.*) I'm sure the young people want to be left alone now . . . let's go into the kitchen, light the oven, kneel down and say a prayer. (*Eddie looks from Ginger to Winnie.*)

WINNIE. Please.

EDDIE. All right . . . but if you need your father, call.

WINNIE. I will. (*Eddie and Ginger exit to the kitchen.*) He's a marvelous man.

SAM. Not for me.

WINNIE. (*Shrugs.*) He's in love with his daughter.

SAM. So am I.

WINNIE. (*Smiles.*) You've got more right . . . but he has priority.

SAM. I suppose. We haven't had much time to talk.

WINNIE. There's nothing to talk about, Sam.

SAM. Too bad about the rabbit . . . (*A pause.*) he died.

WINNIE. You told me on the phone.

SAM. Did I tell you that? I keep forgetting. I guess it's because I want to.

WINNIE. I know.

SAM. What do you think we should do?

WINNIE. I don't know what you're going to do, but I'm going to have my baby.

SAM. A baby . . .

WINNIE. That's right.

SAM. You feel having a baby is the only alternative?

WINNIE. For me.

SAM. Then your father's right . . . I'll get out of music and get into something sane.

WINNIE. Why?

SAM. Well . . . a married man, with a child, should be doing something . . . to make a contribution . . .

WINNIE. Sam . . . you're taking too much for granted.

SAM. What do you mean?

WINNIE. We've been together for three years . . . and we've been perfectly happy . . . but we've never discussed marriage.

SAM. But the rabbit died.

WINNIE. And I'll have the baby, but one thing has nothing to do with the other.

SAM. I don't understand.

WINNIE. I have no intention of marrying you.

SAM. Why not?

WINNIE. Well, first of all, you've never asked me.

SAM. Well . . . there was never any reason before . . .

WINNIE. You see, Sam, I love you and I'm not going to destroy what we have together.

SAM. What does that mean?

WINNIE. You don't really want to get married.

SAM. But . . . but we should . . .

WINNIE. No . . . and I won't have you give up your music and make all the compromises a "married man" must make.

SAM. But it's *my* baby.

WINNIE. (*Smiles.*) No, my darling, instant chauvinist, it's really *our* baby . . . or in the last analysis, *mine*.

SAM. Do you mean you're giving me up?

WINNIE. No, no . . . absolutely not . . . you live at home, do what you have to do and I'll have the baby.

SAM. You mean . . . you want an open relationship.

WINNIE. No, my darling, Sam . . . I'm too liberated to be promiscuous . . . maybe one day we'll be a family, but not right now.

SAM. I refuse to accept this, Winnie!

WINNIE. (*Smiles.*) You have no choice.

SAM. I'll tell your father on you!

WINNIE. It will save me the trouble.

SAM. (*Calls.*) Ed!! . . . Ed!! (*Ginger and Eddie enter from the kitchen.*)

EDDIE. What's going on?

SAM. Your daughter refuses to marry me!

EDDIE. I understand that.

SAM. I mean, pregnant and all, she still refuses to marry me.

EDDIE. Winnie, darling, you can't turn down this idiot.

WINNIE. I have.

GINGER. Why?

WINNIE. Well . . . you see, Mom . . . love is something that two people share and it's marvelous . . . but marriage seems to be a destructive commitment for a woman . . . as soon as two people are *married* the man somehow feels he owns the woman . . . and loses interest.

GINGER. And what are you looking for?

WINNIE. To be loved . . . all the time.

SAM. I'll love you till the day you die, or I die.

WINNIE. That's fine, Sam . . . splendid . . . that's what I want, one man who'll love me all of my life.

SAM. Why does that preclude marriage, Win?

WINNIE. I'm not sure it does . . . but let's wait and see . . . (*Winnie crosses to the staircase.*) I've got to go upstairs and lie down . . . (*She starts up the stairs and turns.*) I feel marvelous, Sam, and full of child. (*Winnie exits up the stairs.*)

SAM. She's crazy, Ed . . .

EDDIE. No . . . no, she's not . . . I know exactly what she means.

SAM. I love her.

EDDIE. She didn't say she didn't love you.

SAM. What should I do?

EDDIE. Go home, Sam . . . I think what my daughter needs is time.

SAM. I don't understand . . . (*Eddie shrugs, helplessly.*)

GINGER. Eventually, maybe, you both will. (*Sam crosses to the arch and turns.*)

SAM. Have I lost her, Ed?

EDDIE. I've no idea.

GINGER. No . . . you haven't lost her . . . she's too much of a woman for that . . . maybe she's lost you for a little while.

SAM. (*Shakes his head.*) But . . . why?

GINGER. It's the new woman's reason, Sam. She doesn't want to belong to a man . . . she wants to be free.

SAM. But she's my woman.

36

GINGER. No . . . she's *her* woman. (*Sam stands and stares at Eddie.*)

EDDIE. I don't understand it, either.

SAM. I've got to go home and think . . . I'll come back later.

GINGER. Call first.

SAM. So long, Ed.

EDDIE. I'll see you, *Son.* (*Sam exits* C., *Offstage, the door slams.*) Poor son-of-a-bitch . . . so my daughter's pregnant and not getting married.

GINGER. No reason she should, if she doesn't want to.

EDDIE. I hope I manage to keep my sanity. (*Eddie sits heavily in his chair.*)

GINGER. Of course you will, it's such a small thing.

EDDIE. It doesn't really matter . . . in view of all that's happened today, I think we can both take consolation in the absolute fact that, the show is never over until the fat lady sings!

GINGER. What in the name of God does that mean?

EDDIE. I'm not operatic, so I have no idea.

GINGER. Darling . . . would you like to get married again?

EDDIE. What do you mean?

GINGER. Just what I said . . .

EDDIE. Why should we re-marry?

GINGER. Well, since you booked the church, the hotel, the flowers and the booze, I think somebody should use them.

EDDIE. Oh, my God, will you fix me a cup of coffee? I think my heart just stopped again. (*Ginger laughs and starts for the kitchen.*) I wish we were Southern, instead of Midwestern. (*Ginger stops and turns at the door.*)

GINGER. Why?

EDDIE. Because, then, all of this would seem normal. (*Ginger laughs and exits to the kitchen. Eddie sits quietly as the curtain falls ending . . .*)

END OF ACT ONE

ACT TWO

Scene 1

TIME: *Later.*
SETTING: *The Same.*
AT RISE: *Ginger comes down the stairs into the living room. As she does, Eddie enters from the kitchen carrying a cup of coffee.*

GINGER. Hi, darling . . . I didn't know you were home.

EDDIE. I just got here.

GINGER. How come you used the back door?

EDDIE. I don't know. I think I'm hiding and I don't even know what I'm hiding from.

GINGER. (*Laughs.*) Disgrace, probably.

EDDIE. Is that what it is?

GINGER. Obviously. You're the father of a pregnant daughter who's not going to get married. Wait 'till that piece of news rocks the town.

EDDIE. You don't seem disturbed at all.

GINGER. I'm not, because I believe in the end, things always work themselves out.

EDDIE. (*Nods.*) Now, you went all through college and studied child psychology, didn't you?

GINGER. That's right.

EDDIE. Has it ever occurred to you that you're a total failure?

GINGER. No, because I think you should lie back and let life pour over you.

EDDIE. I've done that for over twenty years but now it seems the water of life is wearing out my rock.

GINGER. How come you're so late today?

EDDIE. I stopped by the football field. They were scrimmaging . . . and everytime Tink got the ball, the boys on both teams wanted to tackle him. How do you account for that?

GINGER. (*Smiles.*) Easily.

EDDIE. And that doesn't concern you, either?

GINGER. Not at all. You're the one who convinced me it's all

38

over, they'll survive . . . so I'm just going to sit and see how it all comes out.

EDDIE. I'm not sure that I can do that.

GINGER. Good, then you'll be a part of my passing show.

EDDIE. I always knew there was a bit of madness, on your side of the family. Just because I told you something, is no reason for you to believe it. I've been telling you things since you were fourteen years old, and eighty percent of the time I've been wrong.

GINGER. Yes, but think of all the decisions you've saved me. As you know, Eddie, I'm half Irish, and Irish people will believe anything. Any race that believes little people live under mushrooms, has to be touched with madness.

EDDIE. Which reminds me . . . I saw you mad father today.

GINGER. Where?

EDDIE. He was standing in the middle of Main Street, directing traffic.

GINGER. Poor Dad, he always seems to get worse when Mom leaves.

EDDIE. Where did she go?

GINGER. She had to go see my grandmother and grandfather, and try to settle a family crisis.

EDDIE. What's wrong?

GINGER. It seems my grandmother wants a divorce.

EDDIE. A *divorce?* She must be ninety-five years old.

GINGER. Eighty-nine.

EDDIE. They've been married about sixty-five years.

GINGER. Seventy-four.

EDDIE. Seventy-four years?!

GINGER. (*Nods.*) She was fifteen and he was sixteen.

EDDIE. Why would she want a divorce after seventy-four years?

GINGER. Well, she decided she wanted an open relationship, and he refused.

EDDIE. An open relationship, at the age of eighty-nine?! She must be totally crazy!

GINGER. Quite the contrary. She's a very vital, attractive woman. She still drives, plays tennis. She skis . . .

EDDIE. She skis?

GINGER. Of course. The women of the clan have always been very strong. The weakness was in the men.

EDDIE. Your grandmother is eighty-nine years old, wants an open relationship, and skis?

GINGER. That's right.

EDDIE. Is that what I have to look forward to?

GINGER. I've no idea, but women handle time and space better than men.

EDDIE. How?

GINGER. Women have a greater sense of inevitability, they bend with time . . . men generally break because they try to stand up to it. That's why they become impotent . . . and eventually senile.

EDDIE. Since your father seems so happy, I can hardly wait for the second stage.

GINGER. You've got a long way to go before you reach the first stage.

EDDIE. Would you like to take another shot?

GINGER. At what?

EDDIE. Having a baby.

GINGER. Who?

EDDIE. Us.

GINGER. You and me?

EDDIE. That's right.

GINGER. (*Smiles.*) Are you having hot flashes?

EDDIE. In all the wrong places. But, why not? We're both still relatively young. (*Ginger comes to Eddie and clashes into his arms.*) Jesus! I thought if I chased you, you'd run.

GINGER. Those days are gone, my friend.

EDDIE. (*Holds Ginger.*) Wow, that hurt . . . well, what do you say?

GINGER. I'm game if you are. Let's fill the house a second time. Maybe we'll do better. But there's one thing to remember . . . (*Eddie stands and regards Ginger.*) I'm forty-two and you're forty-six. When our new first child is twenty, you'll be sixty-seven years old.

EDDIE. It'll be tough to teach him football.

GINGER. (*Laughs.*) Or anything else.

EDDIE. And that will be just about the time you'll be suggesting an open relationship . . . or a divorce.

GINGER. Possibly, but I just want you to know, I'm available.

EDDIE. Where are the kids right now?

GINGER. Who cares? (*Eddie and Ginger lock in a torrid embrace, as Tinker enters from the kitchen.*)

TINKER. Does anybody care that I have a problem?

40

EDDIE. No. We're no longer concerned with your problems. Your mother and I have decided to have a baby.

TINKER. Don't be ridiculous! Mom would never agree to artificial insemination! (*Eddie glares at Tinker.*)

GINGER. What's wrong, *Tink?*

TINKER. I was just thrown off the football squad.

GINGER. Why?

TINKER. The coach said my presence was too disruptive.

EDDIE. I understand that, it comes down to a question of team morale.

TINKER. In what way?

EDDIE. Well, I think you give the other players a sense of inferiority . . . you see, you're the only tailback I've ever seen who's feet never touch the ground.

TINKER. I don't think that's funny.

EDDIE. I don't either.

TINKER. (*Starts for the kitchen.*) I wish I were five years younger so that I could run away from home.

EDDIE. (*Leaps up.*) You can still run away from home!

TINKER. Where would I go?

EDDIE. Run away to the Army, that's always fun. Then we'll see you again in four years . . . or so . . .

TINKER. They wouldn't accept me, I'm under age.

EDDIE. Your mother and I will run ahead of you and sign the papers.

TINKER. Hmmmm . . . you're kidding but I'd look really neat in those white, tight, sailor pants.

EDDIE. You wouldn't like the Navy.

TINKER. Why not?

EDDIE. Mid-westerners, traditionally, don't like water.

TINKER. Who was thinking of water?

EDDIE. I was.

TINKER. I'm going in the kitchen and fantasize. (*Tinker exits to the kitchen. Eddie stares at Ginger.*)

EDDIE. Is there a circus coming through here soon?

GINGER. They wouldn't buy him.

EDDIE. They're always looking for freaks.

GINGER. Not that freaky . . . he'd frighten the animals . . . no, I wouldn't do that to a circus.

41

EDDIE. Has it occurred to you that we don't seem to like our son very much?

GINGER. Only off and on. And there's nothing wrong with that. Parents and children don't have to like each other all the time. The stress and strain comes from pretending. (*The phone rings. Eddie crosses up to answer. Eddie picks up the phone.*)

EDDIE. Hello . . . just a second, Billie. (*Eddie puts down the phone and crosses L.*) Pick up the phone, Tink.

TINKER. (*Offstage.*) Who is it?

EDDIE. (*Calls.*) Billie!

TINKER. (*Offstage.*) Tell her to get off my case! (*Eddie bangs open the swinging door.*)

EDDIE. Pick up the phone. (*Eddie starts for the phone.*) How did he get to be so rude? (*Eddie hangs up the phone.*)

GINGER. He's a barbarian. We've spawned a character out of the primal nightmare.

EDDIE. Darling, have you ever been unfaithful to me?

GINGER. (*Takes a long beat.*) That's a terrible question to ask. Aren't you ashamed?

EDDIE. Why?

GINGER. Because it's an infringement on the sanctity of the wife-lover relationship . . . *and* . . . and invasion of my civil rights.

EDDIE. I wasn't going to ask you to name names.

GINGER. Then why did you ask?

EDDIE. I hoped, that sometime, you'd had a fling. Like the time you took the European holiday with your mother and father a couple of years after we were married and that you hadn't gone all through life under the same missionary circumstances.

GINGER. That's very sweet.

EDDIE. (*Smiles.*) Yes. A sort of short, wild affair with some conservative Hungarian.

GINGER. I now have the feeling you're getting *too much* vicarious pleasure out of this.

EDDIE. No, it's just if that were true, and properly timed, that maniac outside might not be my son.

GINGER. Oh, he's yours all right. (*The front doorbell rings. Ginger starts for the arch C. She stops and turns.*) But Winnie might not be . . .

EDDIE. The unkindest cut. (*Ginger and Eddie laugh again as Howard Carol, Ginger's father appears in the arch C. Howard is a well pre-*

42

served man in his early seventies who seems to forget things, or not be able to sort out relationships.)

HOWARD. Hello, everybody . . . I'm *home.*

GINGER. Hello, Dad. (*Ginger crosses U. and kisses her father.*)

EDDIE. Hi, Howard, come on in . . . and you are *home.* I hope that's the way you'll always feel about this house.

HOWARD. I certainly will, because I bought it. What the hell are we talking about?

EDDIE. That's a point well taken.

GINGER. Dad, how did you get here?

HOWARD. I jogged.

EDDIE. You *jogged?*

HOWARD. It's only a couple of miles, and whenever Agnes is away, to burn off my energy, I jog every morning and take a lot of cold showers.

EDDIE. Isn't it remarkable that any family could have your grandmother, father, sister and Tink, all alive at the same time . . . four generations of sex maniacs.

GINGER. Eddie!

HOWARD. Eddie's right. I believe everybody should have a vital, happy sex life, as long as they stay away from sheep.

EDDIE. Sheep?

HOWARD. Yes, all that wool makes them much too hot and they're noisy . . .

GINGER. Daddy!

HOWARD. Whereas, if you can catch a fox, right after a forest fire . . .

GINGER. I don't want to hear anymore, Daddy!

HOWARD. I'm only trying to instruct your husband. After all, on his job, he spends a lot of time around farms, and who knows, one day you may decide to take a cruise.

GINGER. That's enough, Daddy!

HOWARD. A fox is much better than another woman. No complications. I was brought up on a farm, Ed, and there was this pretty little black lamb . . .

GINGER. Daddy, why don't you go out into the kitchen and tell this story to Tink. I'm sure he'd love it.

HOWARD. Who?

GINGER. *Tink.*

HOWARD. Who's Tink . . . ?

GINGER. He's your grandson.

43

HOWARD. Then how come I've never seen him?

GINGER. You have seen him.

HOWARD. I don't remember. Is he awfully small?

EDDIE. No, but he's sort of subliminal. He's the one who *flashes* through the room.

HOWARD. Oh, *that* one! Yes, when I was jogging he stopped his car and tried to pick me up . . . and I thought I'd seen him some place, but I couldn't remember where.

GINGER. Why didn't you let him give you a ride?

HOWARD. Well . . . he seemed a little too pushy to me.

GINGER. He's your *grandson!*

HOWARD. Yes, I know. But how many young people say to their grandfather, "How would you like to take a ride, *baby?*"

GINGER. That's just Tink's way of talking.

HOWARD. Well, we athletes can't be too careful. (*The swinging door bursts open and Tinker enters.*)

TINKER. (*Yells.*) She's insane! Totally insane!! I'm going out on the street, and either commit suicide, or run around naked . . . I haven't decided which!

EDDIE. Suicide is better . . . (*Tinker heads for the arch.*)

TINKER. Hello, Gramps, baby.

HOWARD. Hi, sis . . .

EDDIE. (*To Ginger.*) Your father's eyes are getting better. (*Tinker exits through the arch and Offstage the front door is heard to slam. Howard crosses U. to the arch then turns back.*)

HOWARD. Was that him?

EDDIE. That was him.

HOWARD. I think you've got a problem there.

GINGER. His father thinks he's just high spirited.

HOWARD. His father's *sick*. Ask Eddie.

GINGER. Eddie *is* his father, Dad.

HOWARD. Oh. Well, do you know what I'd do with that boy if he was mine? (*Eddie and Ginger stand and wait.*) I'd pack him up and ship him off to Lourdes.

EDDIE. Lourdes, France?

HOWARD. (*Nods.*) I think it's your last hope. They still have some miraculous cures over there. I think it has to do with all those priests and nuns, holding Protestants and Jews under water. It frightens us back to reality. And I think the cure is more effective now since they have a Polish Pope. (*Offstage the doorbell rings. Ginger starts for the arch.*)

44

GINGER. Quite honestly, I don't want to change him so much, that he doesn't seem like one of us. (*Ginger exits through the arch,* C.)

HOWARD. Who?

EDDIE. Tink.

HOWARD. Who's Tink?

EDDIE. I have no idea.

HOWARD. (*Gently.*) He's your *son*, Eddie. Don't try to deny him. (*The puzzled Eddie turns to Howard who is absolutely pleased. Ginger and Sam appear in the arch.*)

EDDIE. Hi, Sam.

SAM. Hello, Ed . . . hello, Mr. Carol. (*Howard stares at Sam.*)

GINGER. Daddy, you remember Sam Graham.

HOWARD. I most certainly do not.

GINGER. Of course you do.

HOWARD. No, I don't.

GINGER. You went to school with his grandfather, they'd just moved here from Georgia, and you developed a whole convoluted theory that if their name was Graham, and they were from Georgia, they must be crackers.

HOWARD. Well, of course! You see, if you simplify things, they're easy to understand. How are you, Tink?

SAM. I'm Sam, Mr. Carol.

HOWARD. What are you doing here?

EDDIE. He's here to see your grandchild.

HOWARD. You don't think he's too old for Tink?

EDDIE. No, no . . . he's engaged in Winnie.

GINGER. *To* Winnie, Ed.

EDDIE. I meant *to*.

HOWARD. Oh, then you're my future great-son-in-law.

SAM. That's my plan. But at the moment it doesn't seem to have much of a future.

HOWARD. I don't seem to know what that means. (*Offstage the front door slams.*)

GINGER. It doesn't mean anything, Dad. (*Winnie appears in the arch* C. *She carries a shopping bag.*)

WINNIE. Hello, everybody. (*Winnie sees Howard and goes to him.*) Well here's my beautiful grandfather. How are you, my darling? (*Winnie reaches up and kisses Howard.*)

HOWARD. How are you, love child?

WINNIE. Much better now that you're here.

SAM. (*Reaches for the shopping bag.*) Let me take that.

WINNIE. I'll do it.

SAM. I'm sorry . . .

WINNIE. (*Crosses* L. *toward kitchen.*) Be right back. Don't go away, darling.

HOWARD. Don't worry, I won't. (*Howard laughs.*) There goes a great girl. And she certainly knows how to get around a man, doesn't she?

GINGER. Oh, yes . . .

EDDIE. She has all kinds of ways.

HOWARD. (*Laughs.*) And I suppose by this time, Sam, you know them all.

SAM. No, she discovered a whole new way to get around me, and the last I knew she was headed that way . . . (*Sam points to the kitchen.*)

HOWARD. Well, the engagement period is the worst time, and the first year of marriage isn't much good for the man. But I promise you, women become completely dependent, as soon as they discover they're pregnant.

SAM. That's good to know.

EDDIE. I suggest you tell that rule to Winnie, Sam.

GINGER. Right after the engagement's over. (*Winnie enters from the kitchen.*)

WINNIE. I don't want to alarm anybody, but Tink is dancing on the front lawn in his jockey shorts.

GINGER. That's all right, it keeps him off the streets.

EDDIE. And maybe he'll get pneumonia . . .

WINNIE. Did you tell Grandfather my good news?

GINGER. (*Quickly.*) We told him you were engaged.

WINNIE. That's all?

EDDIE. If you want to tell him anything else, let's call the paramedics first. I'm no good at heart attacks.

WINNIE. (*Smiles.*) I think Grandfather can handle it.

EDDIE. I'm talking about me.

WINNIE. (*To Howard.*) Darling, do you believe that men are more equal than women?

HOWARD. No, I believe that man or woman, everybody should be allowed to do what they want to do. I live by the philosophy of Saint Augustine, who said, "Love God, but do as you please."

WINNIE. And you always encouraged your three daughters to do as they pleased?

HOWARD. I encouraged your mother when she went out for the boys high school football team. Didn't I ever tell you that story?!

EDDIE. Yes, you have!

GINGER. Thousands of times!

WINNIE. (*Ecstatic.*) Tell it again, Grandfather, I don't think Sam's ever heard it, and he's a little confused about Women's Rights. (*Howard is on his feet like a tiger.*)

HOWARD. It was the last play of the last game of the season! The enemy had the ball, it was fourth down and ten to go, they had to kick! Suddenly the whistle blows. Our team calls a time out. They go back into a huddle. The fans sense something momentous is going to happen. One man breaks away from the huddle and starts toward the bench. It's Eddie Davis, the captain! (*Howard points to Eddie.*) The crowd cheers. You were pretty good that day . . .

EDDIE. Thanks, Dad.

HOWARD. But who are they putting in his place?

WINNIE. Who?

HOWARD. My daughter! She trots away from the bench across the field. The fans go mad. They scream, they whistle, they cheer. They're yelling, "It's her, It's her!" I am completely calm and silent.

SAM. I'm sure.

HOWARD. The referee greets her, she greets him. She joins the circle of her teammates. They're glad she's in the game.

GINGER. Daddy, get to the play.

HOWARD. Don't you want the mood.

GINGER. No.

HOWARD. Okay. Fourth and ten. They're going back to kick. My daughter is sent back to the safety position to receive the punt. The ball is snapped. He gets the kick away. It's a long one down the field, past the fifty-yard line. She's going back, back! She takes it in her own territory and starts up the field. The ends try to box her in, but she slips them and starts for the right side. The crowd is on its feet, she shakes off a tackler at the thirty-five. She's down to the thirty, and is *trapped*.

SAM. (*Caught up.*) Big boys?

HOWARD. Reverse your field, I scream. Reverse your field! She hears me! She cuts back to the thirty-five, swings over to the left side, crosses back to the center and streaks off into the clear, with only three men between her and the goal line.

SAM. *Three men?*

HOWARD. They start up after her. They think they've got her in

47

a trap. But she doesn't yield. She tries to feint them out of position but they keep coming. Suddenly she does a half spin, straight arms a man, hurdles the man who tries to knock her out of bounds and then dances down the sideline stripe and over the goal line for a touchdown. Pay dirt! And after it was over, the whole team led by Captain Eddie Davis, boosted her up on their shoulders, carried her around the field, and I led the snake dance. (*Howard hugs Eddie and Ginger.*) What a day and what a game! I was exhausted! And that's the way it was, darling Winnie.

WINNIE. (*Kisses Howard.*) Beautiful, Grandfather, you're a *marvel.*

HOWARD. I know, and now I've got to get back home.

EDDIE. I'll drive you.

HOWARD. No, no, after that play, I've got to jog. (*Howard crosses U. to the arch and turns.*) And if I find a fox along the way, I'll save her for you! (*Howard waves and exits. Eddie shakes his head.*)

EDDIE. I've heard that story five hundred times, and he never leaves out a word.

GINGER. I'm going to have it chiseled on his tombstone.

WINNIE. That would make him very happy.

SAM. (*To Ginger.*) And is it true? Did you really play football with boys?

EDDIE. Oh, yeah!

SAM. Well, that explains a lot of things . . .

WINNIE. The only interesting incident in that story is, when my mother did something unconventional . . . the two people who were most understanding and supportive, were her father . . . (*Winnie turns and looks at Eddie.*) and the young man she eventually married . . . (*Winnie turns and stares at Sam.*) maybe that's something we should all think about. (*Offstage the front door slams.*)

EDDIE. Maybe there's something else *you* should think about. (*Billie appears in the arch, C.*)

BILLIE. Mr. Davis, Tink just called me. He's run away from home.

EDDIE. Good.

BILLIE. Aren't you going to call the police?

EDDIE. No. They might find him.

BILLIE. I'll go and look for him. (*Billie races Off. There's a pause, then the door Offstage slams, to punctuate the moment.*)

WINNIE. (*Quietly.*) What is the *something* I should think about?

EDDIE. Responsibility.

48

WINNIE. To whom?

EDDIE. To your mother, Sam, me.

WINNIE. I'm only responsible to my child and myself.

EDDIE. That's a very kindless thing to say in front of Sam.

WINNIE. (*Turns to Sam.*) It's true.

SAM. Your father's right. I'm not going to stand by forever.

WINNIE. Perhaps it's best you don't stand by at all.

SAM. You must understand, as a man, there are certain adjustments I can't make.

WINNIE. I haven't asked you to. Go home, Sam.

SAM. You do understand.

WINNIE. No.

SAM. (*Crosses* U. *to the arch.*) I'll call you later.

WINNIE. I may not be here later. (*Sam waves to Eddie and Ginger and exits. The front door closes Offstage.*)

EDDIE. You're ruthless, Win . . .

WINNIE. Why? Because I want to be my own person?

EDDIE. It's the time of me and self, isn't it?

WINNIE. No, I want to share my life, but I don't want to *belong* to anybody else.

EDDIE. I never thought I'd hear that remark made by a child of mine.

WINNIE. I know. But none of us can live in your image, since you think of yourself as perfect.

EDDIE. What? (*Winnie stands and looks at her father a long beat, then turns and exits up the stairs. Eddie turns to Ginger.*)

GINGER. She's right. (*Eddie moves closer to Ginger.*)

EDDIE. I think I've become the victim of truth. (*Ginger smiles, places her arms about her husband and holds him, as the curtain falls, ending . . .*)

END OF SCENE 1

ACT TWO

SCENE 2

TIME: *Two days later.*
SETTING: *The same.*
AT RISE: *The stage is uninhabited. In the arch* C. *there stands a*

steamer trunk and two large pieces of luggage. The kitchen door swings and Eddie enters, carrying the inevitable mug of coffee. Eddie glances toward the arch, the trunk catches his eye. He crosses up to the arch and regards the luggage for a long moment, nods his head, then turns and crosses back to the living room proper. Offstage the front doorbell rings. Eddie looks toward the sound, shakes his head "no" and turns away. Offstage the front door is heard to open and close. Eddie turns back toward the sound and waits. In a moment Howard appears in the arch.

HOWARD. Hello, Ed.

EDDIE. Hi, Howard.

HOWARD. Weren't you going to answer the door?

EDDIE. No, because I said to myself, if it's trouble; I am not at home. And if it's family, they'll just come in.

HOWARD. Being one of the family, doesn't mean it's not trouble.

EDDIE. Especially in this family.

HOWARD. (*Indicates the luggage.*) You planning a trip?

EDDIE. No. Your granddaughter's moving out today. She decided she no longer wanted to live at home. It's the end of an era.

HOWARD. (*Smiles.*) That's a very fancy thought, but both parental and subjective. However, from her point of view, it might be the beginning of an era.

EDDIE. I've spent twenty-one years with her, I can't be that objective.

HOWARD. (*Almost laughs.*) The next cliche is, "the best years of my life."

EDDIE. You're not leaving me much room for self pity.

HOWARD. I suppose what most of us would like, is to have our children stay home and not get married until we died. Then, no matter how old they were, have them go out and start a life of their own.

EDDIE. No, but twenty-one is awfully young.

HOWARD. You didn't think that when you married my daughter.

EDDIE. I wish I were in a bar, talking to a stranger.

HOWARD. He wouldn't even listen. And don't be depressed, Ed, all fathers feel the same way. It's called temporary melancholia.

EDDIE. When does it end? (*Offstage the front door opens and closes.*)

HOWARD. It never ends. I still don't like you for stealing my daughter away. (*Eddie and Howard smile as Ginger appears c.*)

EDDIE. Hello, my darling wife.

GINGER. Hello, Ed . . . hi, Daddy.

HOWARD. Hello, there . . .

GINGER. I'm your daughter.

HOWARD. No, Ed just explained to me *you're* his wife, not *my* daughter because once a daughter rejects a father for another man . . .

GINGER. (*Cuts in.*) I don't want to hear anymore of *that* ghastly conversation. (*Ginger indicates the luggage.*) I see Winnie is still here.

EDDIE. Were you hoping she'd be gone?

GINGER. She's only moving six blocks away.

EDDIE. She's leaving my house. (*Eddie turns and crosses away. Howard smiles.*)

GINGER. Oh, boy . . . (*Ginger turns to Howard.*) Did you jog out here?

HOWARD. No, I got a ride. Your mother's coming home tonight. I'm meeting her at the airport, so I've got to be rested.

GINGER. Did she manage to work that situation out?

HOWARD. Oh, yes. You're mother effected a compromise. My folks are not getting a divorce. From now on, they're taking separate holidays, three times a year, and no questions asked.

EDDIE. Who'll push her wheelchair?

HOWARD. If I know my mother, she'll find somebody, or have a motor installed. (*Howard sits in the chair R.C.*)

EDDIE. For an open relationship, at eighty-nine, she'll need a motor installed in more than the wheelchair. (*Howard laughs, puts his head back and closes his eyes.*)

GINGER. Any news about Tink?

HOWARD. Who's Tink?

GINGER. Your grandson . . . the one who ran away.

HOWARD. Funny, I can never remember who that is. My God, that Second World War was exciting. I remember landing on the beach at Normandy and driving through to Paris. All the French girls waving and throwing flowers . . . (*He seems to relive the moment then sits and snuggles back in the chair and drifts off.*)

EDDIE. Tink and Billie are on their way here.

GINGER. With a police escort?

EDDIE. No, they were released in their own recognizance.

GINGER. Do you realize that yesterday was Tink's seventeenth birthday?

EDDIE. And I should think it's the one he'll never forget, since he spent it in a motel with an absolutely gorgeous, sixteen-year-old girl. I can picture the whole scene. Billie saying, "Tink, darling, you'll never guess what I'm going to give you for your birthday." And my son saying, "It's very pretty, but what do you do with it?"

GINGER. And to think, at sixteen, I was still skipping rope. (*Winnie is seen coming down the stairs.*)

WINNIE. Mom. (*Ginger holds her finger to her lips and indicates the sleeping Howard.*) Is he all right?

GINGER. Just tired. Are you about ready?

WINNIE. Just about. But I need somebody to help me get that trunk in the station wagon. (*Ginger turns to Eddie. He stands and stares implacably. He's not going to help.*)

GINGER. (*Turns back to Winnie.*) I guess we're going to have to call a moving man.

EDDIE. I'm going to get more coffee. (*Eddie turns abruptly, and exits to the kitchen.*)

WINNIE. It seems I no longer have a man in my life.

GINGER. Well, maybe you'll have a son, and you can program him to react exactly the way you think he should. (*Ginger turns toward the kitchen.*) I've got to go and have a summit meeting with your father. (*Winnie stands for a long moment, wanders about and crosses to Howard. She stands behind the chair and in search of a man, she reaches down and strokes his face.*)

WINNIE. Beautiful grandfather . . . (*Howard wakes and doesn't know quite where he is.*)

HOWARD. Is it time . . . ? (*He glances up and sees Winnie.*) Oh, when you stroked me, I thought it was forty years ago, and you were my Agnes.

WINNIE. I wish both things were true.

HOWARD. (*Smiles.*) I was cock of the walk then . . . married to the most beautiful woman in the world . . . small children running through the house . . . I believed in immortality . . . now . . . (*Howard raises his hands in a gesture of helplessness. Winnie sits on the ottoman.*)

WINNIE. You'll always be immortal.

HOWARD. No . . . all things in the realm of time must end, except time . . . and maybe love . . . love seems infinite.

WINNIE. What's finite?

HOWARD. Life.

WINNIE. I'm lonely.

HOWARD. And confused?

WINNIE. No. I know exactly what I want. But nobody seems to see it my way.

HOWARD. I know I could never deal with my parents either. When we visited them last year, I got into a discussion and my mother tried to send me to my room. (*Winnie and Howard both laugh. Winnie places her head in Howard's lap.*)

WINNIE. Tell me what to do.

HOWARD. Age and wisdom are two separate things.

WINNIE. I hurt.

HOWARD. (*Nods.*) Pain, little darling, isn't always bad. Do you love Sam?

WINNIE. Yes.

HOWARD. Then go with him . . .

WINNIE. I can't. He wants to marry me for all the wrong reasons.

HOWARD. I didn't say marry him, I said go with him.

WINNIE. I never thought I'd hear you say that . . .

HOWARD. I once said it to your mother . . . (*They both sit for a long moment.*) The only piece of advice I have for you is don't betray your life for the sake of pride . . . or principle. (*Howard rises from the chair.*) And Winnie, don't judge anybody too harshly because he strays from the paths of righteousness. The only spark of divinity left in man is his capacity to forgive. (*Howard reaches over and holds onto the back of the chair.*) I'm suddenly very dizzy.

WINNIE. (*Jumps up.*) I think you should come upstairs and take a nap.

HOWARD. I think you're right.

WINNIE. (*Calls.*) Mom! (*Ginger enters from the kitchen.*) I'm taking grandfather upstairs.

GINGER. Are you all right, Dad? (*Eddie enters from the kitchen.*)

HOWARD. Fine . . . fine . . . just a little dizzy . . . (*Winnie and Howard start for the stairs.*)

WINNIE. He wants to take a nap.

EDDIE. I'll take him up. (*Winnie turns and says sharply.*)

WINNIE. No . . . I'll take him up. (*Eddie and Winnie stare at each other.*)

EDDIE. Do as you please . . . you always do anyway.

WINNIE. That's right! (*Winnie glares at her father, then turns away. She and Howard exit up the stairs.*)

GINGER. There was no reason for that.

EDDIE. She's willfull . . .

GINGER. Cut the ties and let her drift from you, Eddie, there's no other way . . .

EDDIE. I'm not trying to hold her . . . I just wish she'd be more civilized. (*Offstage the door is heard to open and close.*)

53

GINGER. You mean like you . . . (*Tinker and Billie appear in the arch. This is not the same two young people that have been seen, in any previous scene. They are not only subdued by their experience of the past two days, but they are, as well, rather formally dressed. Tinker wears a blue blazer, grey slacks and a shirt and tie. Billie is garbed in an attractive dress, a light fall coat and perhaps a very chic hat.*)

TINKER. Hello, Mom . . . Dad . . . (*Billie puts up a hand and waves embarrassed.*)

BILLIE. Hi . . .

GINGER. How are you, Tink?

TINKER. Fine.

GINGER. That's good.

TINKER. I'm sorry.

BILLIE. I'm not.

EDDIE. I like that about women.

TINKER. I guess you're pretty mad.

EDDIE. Well that's a condition I've lived with most of my married life.

TINKER. I just want you to know it was all my fault.

BILLIE. No, it wasn't, Tinker, don't be a credit grabber.

TINKER. You see, I planned it for a long time . . . that's why I acted so crazy . . . you know . . . made believe I wasn't wild for Billie . . . pretended to be gay . . . got myself thrown off the football team . . . I even packed these clothes, so that when we split we'd look older, and I had fake I.D.'s made. I never thought we'd be caught.

EDDIE. Well, as a father, I have only one disappointment about you and Billie.

TINKER. What's that?

EDDIE. That you didn't end up as Bonnie and Clyde.

GINGER. Listen to me, Tink . . .

EDDIE. Listen to your mother . . .

GINGER. I think you've gotten enough mileage out of this attention-getting caper. As far as your father and I are concerned, it's over, and no longer discussable. Now . . . why don't you take Billie home, and face the symphony next door?

TINKER. Okay.

BILLIE. Could we stay here for a little while and relax, we're both exhausted . . . jail is hell.

GINGER. Sure. I'll call your parents and tell them you're here. (*Ginger crosses to the phone.*)

54

BILLIE. Thanks. (*Tinker and Billie start for the stairs.*)

EDDIE. Where are you going?

TINKER. We're going to bed.

EDDIE. What are you talking about?

BILLIE. I told you we were exhausted.

EDDIE. Get back here, and lie down on the floor!

TINKER. Why?

EDDIE. Because you're not going to bed together in *this* house.

TINKER. But we're married. (*Ginger hangs down the phone.*)

GINGER. You're what?

EDDIE. (*Nods in despair.*) The wrong kid got married.

GINGER. Who'd marry you?

BILLIE. Me.

GINGER. No, no . . . who married you, and how did it happen?

BILLIE. A judge.

TINKER. We had forged blood tests, drivers' licenses, and marriage certificates.

GINGER. Why?

TINKER. Because we knew if we told you, you wouldn't let us get married.

EDDIE. So now you have a forged marriage.

TINKER. I don't agree.

BILLIE. We're married in the eyes of God.

EDDIE. Well, God and I have different eyes. Go sleep in his bedroom. You're not going to sleep here.

TINKER. I never objected when you and Mom went to bed together.

EDDIE. That's the kind of logic that makes parents old . . . old . . . *old* . . .

TINKER. Very well then, let's put everything in its proper perspective.

EDDIE. I can hardly wait.

TINKER. No matter what either you, or Billie's parents think, Billie and I are man and wife. If you, or they, elect to try and annul our marriage, a year from now, when I'm eighteen and she's seventeen, we'll get married again.

GINGER. And her father will annul it again.

TINKER. The inevitable can only be postponed, not changed. We have made our decision. We have decided what we are going to do with our lives. (*The pretentious pronouncement over, Tinker turns to Billie.*) Let's go and inform your father and mother.

BILLIE. Yes, husband.

TINKER. (*To Ginger and Eddie.*) Thank you for your understanding. Perhaps we'll see you later and perhaps we won't. Come, wife. (*Tinker turns and exits through the arch.*)

BILLIE. Bye, Mom . . . Dad . . . (*Billie crosses to the arch and turns.*) Isn't he masterful! (*Billie laughs and exits.*)

GINGER. Well, *husband,* what parental attitude are we going to strike?

EDDIE. I don't even want to discuss it. All I can tell you is, that I liked him better when he wanted to experiment. Now he's just middle class, and dreary.

GINGER. You mean you'd have preferred to have a son who was interesting, and in a mental institution?

EDDIE. No, no, not in an institution. But committable.

GINGER. I think he's more committable now than he was three days ago. There's nothing wrong with wanting to fly. But any boy who gets married at seventeen can't be mentally well.

EDDIE. Should we have it annuled?

GINGER. I don't see why . . .

EDDIE. Billie is sixteen years old.

GINGER. So was my grandmother when she got married . . . and you're the one who wanted a whole new family . . .

EDDIE. I meant you and me.

GINGER. And Tink is right . . . why try to postpone it . . . ?

EDDIE. Suppose it doesn't work?

GINGER. For a woman, it's better to find that out at sixteen than thirty.

EDDIE. Then your vote is with them?

GINGER. If we tall people have any brains, we'll all vote with them, if that's what they want, which I doubt . . . otherwise, their act of love wil become a shabby little thing.

EDDIE. They're still in high school.

GINGER. How marvelous.

EDDIE. Where will they live?

GINGER. It doesn't matter. I'm sure the truth is they're only playing a game . . . but if we oppose them, they'll insist.

EDDIE. You're right. If that's what they want, let's support them. They might set an example for the girl upstairs.

GINGER. Don't do that . . . you might drive them away as well. (*Offstage the front door slams.*)

EDDIE. Okay. (*Sam appears in the arch* C. *He's furious.*)

56

SAM. I'm furious and I've had it!

GINGER. Will you excuse me, I'm going to the kitchen, to avoid this discussion. (*Ginger exits to the kitchen.*)

EDDIE. What's today's problem, Sam?

SAM. She's moving out today!

EDDIE. I know.

SAM. She's my wife, Ed!

EDDIE. No, she's not.

SAM. I'm the father of her child.

EDDIE. I hope you're right.

SAM. Oh, please, don't do that to me, Ed . . . she *has* to marry me.

EDDIE. No, she doesn't.

SAM. Do you mean that all these years she's just been using me?

EDDIE. Well . . . I think . . . even though she took *advantage* of you . . . she still respects you. However, I believe she feels she's too young to get married and settle down. She'd like to have other experiences. (*Eddie stands and stares at Sam.*)

SAM. She can't do that to me.

EDDIE. (*Explodes.*) What the hell are we talking about?!

SAM. What do you mean?

EDDIE. Stop being irrational!

SAM. That's the first time you've yelled at me since I was thirteen years old.

EDDIE. Because you're acting like a virginal, sixteen-year-old girl, instead of a man . . . "Has she just been using me?" What kind of nonsense is that?

SAM. Well . . . has she? . . . I'm sorry . . . but I'm in love with her.

EDDIE. Then go and tell her you're in love with her . . . hold her . . . be gentle and understanding, and show her some tenderness . . . that's what every woman needs at a time like this.

SAM. Men too . . .

EDDIE. Take her in your arms, tell her she's your girl, and whatever she does is all right with you. (*Sam stands and contemplates the thought.*)

SAM. No.

EDDIE. No?

SAM. (*Shakes his head.*) You're wrong. (*Eddie stands and nods his head.*) Our relationship is not predicated on that kind of dishon-

57

esty. When she comes down, I'm going to be direct and firm, and explain to her that she, the child and I, are a family unit. From now on, I will accept all of the responsibility for that unit; because I am the man, the father, and the head of the family.

EDDIE. (*Nods.*) Would you rather be buried or cremated? (*Eddie crosses to the stairs and calls.*) Winnie!

WINNIE. (*Offstage.*) Yes!

EDDIE. Come down . . . I have a surprise for you. You have a visitor who says he is a man. (*Eddie turns and starts* L.) Winnie is about one-sixteenth Irish.

SAM. What does that mean?

EDDIE. They're savages. You cross her and she'll tear you tooth from claw! (*Eddie exits to the kitchen. Sam crosses* R. *toward the window, as Winnie appears on the staircase.*)

WINNIE. Hello, Sam. Are you the surprise?

SAM. I guess so.

WINNIE. Thanks for coming over to help me move.

SAM. You're not going to move.

WINNIE. I'm not?

SAM. No.

WINNIE. Tell me about it.

SAM. I intend to do more than just *tell* you about it! I've taken about all I'm going to take from you, Win, and this is where I draw the line. From now on, you will listen to me, and you will respect what I have to say. (*Winnie stares and stands absolutely still.*) You are not going to leave this house and you are not going to move into that apartment . . . you and I are going to discuss this like civilized human beings, and when we get everything settled, we are going to be married in a proper ceremony. Do you understand?

WINNIE. (*Quietly.*) No.

SAM. Good. All through our relationship, we've always been relatively honest with each other, but it seems that ever since you've discovered you were pregnant, you've gone off half cocked, and reason and logic doesn't work with you anymore. So I've decided we're going to forego any further discussion, and do things my way.

WINNIE. Really—

SAM. Because now you've become both devious and dishonest, and I'm not going to tolerate it.

WINNIE. Devious and dishonest.

58

SAM. Yes, you didn't tell me you planned parenthood.

WINNIE. I couldn't have done it without you.

SAM. And you didn't tell me you intended to move out of here.

WINNIE. Sam . . . Sam, we've talked about that for years.

SAM. Of course. But we said *someday* we'll move out and get married and have children . . . but that was just *talk*.

WINNIE. For me, it's not talk anymore.

SAM. And you never said you didn't plan to marry me.

WINNIE. I still haven't said that?

SAM. When? (*Winnie holds a beat and almost smiles.*)

WINNIE. Do you know what I'm going to do with you?

SAM. Marry me.

WINNIE. No.

SAM. (*Panics.*) You're not going to get rid of me . . . listen, I didn't really mean all those things I said about you being devious and dishonest . . . you know how neurotic I am . . . I'm a musician . . . It was a conversation I made up last night when I couldn't sleep, but it didn't work out the way I thought it would . . .

WINNIE. Those conversations never do.

SAM. What are you going to do with me?

WINNIE. I'm going to compromise you, Sam. (*Sam stands and waits.*) You can come to my flat whenever you want, and stay as long as you like . . . till you're fully weaned away from your family, and not afraid of life anymore. And we'll both do what we *want* to do and *have* to do. Then maybe we'll discuss marriage but only *maybe*.

SAM. I'm not sure that's what I want.

WINNIE. (*Smiles.*) Well it doesn't matter, it's either that, or nothing at all . . .

SAM. Nothing matters to me, except you. I love you . . . and whatever you want is what you'll have.

WINNIE. That's very sweet and tender, Sam . . . now go and put the things in the car.

SAM. All right, darling. (*Sam crosses up through the arch and picks up the two heavy suitcases.*)

WINNIE. (*Calls upstairs.*) Ready, Grandfather?

HOWARD. (*Offstage.*) In a minute.

WINNIE. (*Calls toward the kitchen.*) Bye, Mom . . . (*Sam exits with the suitcases. Ginger and Eddie enter from the kitchen.*)

GINGER. You ready to go?

WINNIE. All set. (*Ginger looks from Winnie to Eddie, wondering which one will yield.*)

GINGER. Who's taking care of the luggage?

WINNIE. Sam.

GINGER. I'd best go help, I've never trusted gong warmers. (*Ginger turns and exits through the arch. Winnie and Eddie are left alone on stage. They stand and face each other a moment.*)

EDDIE. If I hadn't come out of the kitchen, you'd have left without saying goodbye.

WINNIE. Are you going to let me go without your blessings?

EDDIE. You'll go with or without them.

WINNIE. Yes, I will. (*Winnie holds a beat then starts to turn.*)

EDDIE. Fathers and daughters . . . (*Winnie turns back to her father.*) we're disappointed when we have them and heart broken when we lose them. (*Eddie drifts away.*) Especially when there's another man involved. (*Eddie stands a long moment.*) I'm a fool. I didn't want you to leave for all the wrong reasons. (*Winnie stands and watches.*) I didn't want to lose you. I was thinking of my happiness, not yours . . . that's the truth. But now I realize the only love that should grow toward separation is the love of a parent for a child.

WINNIE. I love you. (*Winnie comes toward Eddie. He holds her tenderly.*)

EDDIE. You'd . . . better . . .

WINNIE. Go . . . I know . . . (*Winnie turns and exits. Eddie watches her off and stands quietly.*)

HOWARD. (*Offstage, calls.*) Winnie! Don't leave without me! (*Howard starts down the steps.*)

EDDIE. Would you like me to take you home?

HOWARD. No, I don't like the way you drive, never have . . .

EDDIE. Would you like Virginia to take you to the airport later?

HOWARD. No, I'd rather meet my wife alone . . . she may be in heat . . . (*Eddie shakes his head in disbelief, and moves away, as Sam appears and starts for the trunk.*)

EDDIE. Do you want me to give you a hand with that, Sam?

SAM. No, thanks. I'm accustomed to carrying drums. (*Sam swings the trunk up on his back and carries it off.*)

HOWARD. I'm glad for Winnie that he's got a strong back.

EDDIE. Are you all right, Howard?

60

HOWARD. Fine . . . why?

EDDIE. You didn't seem too well earlier . . .

HOWARD. I know. But when you reach my age, Ed, you'll realize that nobody pays you much attention unless you act a little faint from time to time, or behave a little peculiar.

EDDIE. What do you mean?

HOWARD. (*Smiles.*) Just what I said . . .

EDDIE. You mean . . . you've been putting everybody on for the past few years?

HOWARD. Of course . . . I'm as physically and mentally sound as you are. Sometimes I think more sound.

EDDIE. Well, you old reprobate!

HOWARD. Don't give my secret away, Ed . . . you can use it after I'm gone. (*Howard crosses up to the arch.*) You can't imagine the laughs I've had . . . especially about Tink . . . I know who Tink is, always have, he's a friend of Peter Pan's . . . (*Howard exits. Eddie somewhat puzzled moves D.L. as Ginger enters, stands a beat, almost smiles and says.*)

GINGER. Well, the end of another wrenching crisis.

EDDIE. Not really.

GINGER. I know. You never really did care much for a family crisis you could stare down.

EDDIE. The shock wasn't so much with your daughter, as with your father.

GINGER. I'm worried about him.

EDDIE. (*Almost smiles.*) I'm sure you are.

GINGER. He's getting frail, and more forgetful . . . (*Eddie stands and nods.*) He just said, "I think I'll drive" and got into the back seat of the car. (*Eddie watches and almost laughs.*) It's not funny . . . we're going to have to pay a lot more attention to Dad.

EDDIE. I know I am. (*Eddie wanders to the chair* C., *but doesn't sit as yet. The late afternoon sun sims slightly. Eddie glances about.*) Is it getting dark in here?

GINGER. A little dusky. Would you like some coffee?

EDDIE. (*Turns.*) What?

GINGER. Some coffee?

EDDIE. Oh . . . no, thank you. (*Eddie looks toward the window.*) It's getting late, darling.

GINGER. Not really. (*Eddie sits heavily in his chair.*) I just helped

Dad and Winnie load the wagon and thought, "Three generations . . . and a fourth not very far off . . ." So it seems that nothing in life is ever really finished. (*Eddie simply stares out front.*)

EDDIE. I suppose not.

GINGER. Then coming up the walk, I stopped and watched Billie and Tink, romping around on the lawn next door, like kids. (*Eddie continues to stare out front.*)

EDDIE. And very soon, we'll be alone.

GINGER. No. Tink will be back here in a very short time. (*Eddie doesn't face Ginger.*) Did you hear what I said?

EDDIE. What? . . . no . . . I guess not.

GINGER. I said Tink will be back home, in a very short time. (*Eddie sits and stares at Ginger a long moment, then says.*)

EDDIE. Who's Tink? (*Eddie turns back front and stares vacuously. Ginger starts to cross toward Eddie very slowly in an effort to determine whether or not Eddie is putting her on. Eddie smiles benignly as . . . the curtain falls ending . . .*)

THE END

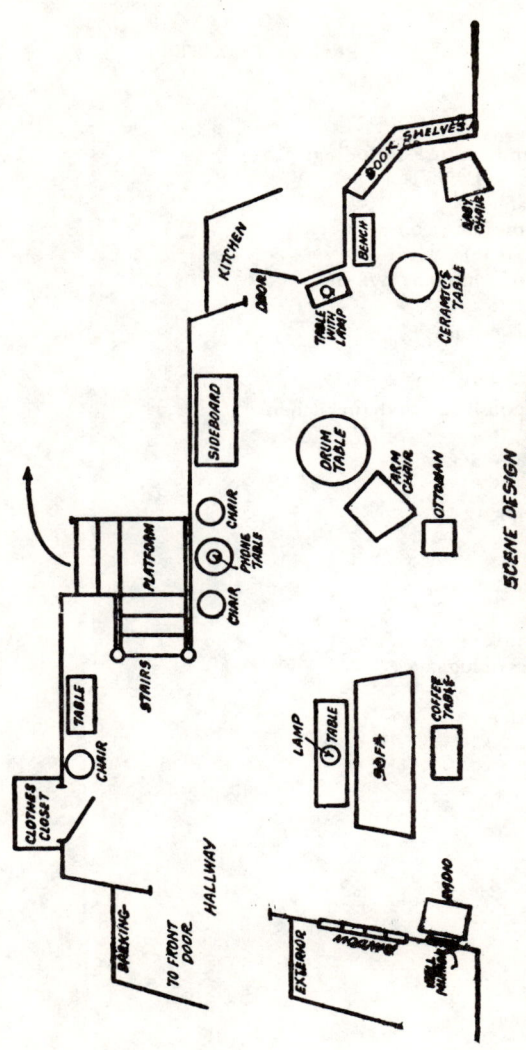

SCENE DESIGN

TIME AND GINGER

PROPERTY LIST

ACT ONE
On Stage
living room furniture, including:
    sofa
    coffee table } (D.R.C.)
    large arm chair (L.C.)
    ottoman (L.C.)
curtains, to be hung by WINNIE
telephone
assorted magazines
Offstage
attache case (GINGER)
furniture polish and cloth (in kitchen)

ACT TWO—SCENE 1
Offstage
cup of coffee
shopping bag

ACT TWO—SCENE 2
On Stage
steamer trunk
large pieces of luggage (2)
Offstage
mug of coffee

New
PLAYS

THE 5TH OF JULY

LANDSCAPE OF THE BODY

THE NIGHT OF THE TRIBADES

OLD MAN JOSEPH AND HIS FAMILY

ULYSSES IN TRACTION

THE MANDRAKE

HOOTERS

THE WAYSIDE MOTOR INN

COUNTING THE WAYS & LISTENING

PATIO/PORCH

AH, EURYDICE!

Inquiries Invited

DRAMATISTS PLAY SERVICE, INC.

440 Park Avenue South   New York, N. Y. 10016

RECENT

Releases . . .

ON GOLDEN POND
CURSE OF THE STARVING CLASS
BOSOMS AND NEGLECT
TAKEN IN MARRIAGE
THE MIGHTY GENTS
BODIES
A VOICE OF MY OWN
A CHRISTMAS CAROL:
   SCROOGE AND MARLEY
WINTER CHICKEN
THE UNINVITED
MY CUP RANNETH OVER
   (One Act)

*Write for information as to
availability*